PRAYING BY HAND

BY THE SAME AUTHOR

Called
New Thinking on Christian Vocation

Daily We Touch Him
Practical Religious Experiences

Centering Prayer
*Renewing an Ancient Christian
Prayer Form*

Centered Living
The Way of Centering Prayer

A Place Apart
*Monastic Prayer and Practice
for Everyone*

Monastic Journey to India

Eucharist Yesterday and Today

In Peter's Footsteps
Learning to Be a Disciple

Jubilee
A Monk's Journal

O Holy Mountain
Journal of a Retreat on Mount Athos

In Search of True Wisdom
*Visits to Eastern Spiritual
Fathers and Mothers*

Challenges in Prayer

Monastery

Last of the Fathers

Breaking Bread
The Table Talk of Jesus

A Manual of Life
The New Testament for Daily Reading

Mary Today
*Challenging Woman, Model
for Maturing Christians*

Thomas Merton, Brother Monk
The Quest for True Freedom

Daily We Follow Him
Learning Discipleship from Peter

Prayertimes: Morning, Midday,
Evening
*A Pocket "Liturgy of the Hours"
for All Christians*

A Retreat with Thomas Merton

Living Our Priesthood Today

Through the Year with the Saints
*A Daily Companion for Private
or Liturgical Prayer*

Long on the Journey
The Reflections of a Pilgrim

Call to the Center
*The Gospel's Invitation to Deeper
Prayer*

Light from the Cloister

The Monastic Way

The Way of the Cistercians

Praying By Hand

Rediscovering the Rosary as a Way of Prayer

125 7679

M. Basil Pennington, O.C.S.O.

242.74
PEN.

 HarperSanFrancisco
A Division of HarperCollins*Publishers*

FIRST EDITION

Library of Congress Cataloging-in-Publication Data

Pennington, M. Basil.
   The rosary / M. Basil Pennington.
     p.   cm.
   Includes bibliographical references.
   ISBN 0–06–066508–4
   1. Rosaries.   2. Beads—Religious aspects—Catholic Church.   3. Catholic Church—Doctrines.   I. Title.
   BX2310.R7P46   1991
   241'.74—dc20
                                                          90–55775
                                                              CIP

94   95   RRD(H)   10   9   8   7   6   5   4   3   2

This edition is printed on acid-free paper that meets the American National Standards Institute Z39.48 Standard.

To
Saint Anne
the mother of the mother of God
and
to the memory of
Helen Cecile Kenny,
my grandmother,
and of all the grandmothers
who have taught little ones how to pray
more by example than by word,
who have been part of
the living tradition
that has passed on
the rosary

Contents

Preface: The Beads

The beads! I hold in my hand a very humble little rosary. These beads, once white, have turned green over the years. Some of them, broken or lost, have been replaced by black ones. The chain has lost any luster it might once have had. The original cross, too, has been replaced by a small black plastic one of Byzantine style. It is certainly not much to look at, this rosary. But it is precious to me. Over thirty years ago it was blessed by Pope John XXIII of saintly memory, and it was blessed again by Pope Paul VI on the very day of his election as pope. It has been touched to Calvary's rock, to the stone in Bethlehem's grotto, and to the relics of innumerable saints. It was in my hand when I knelt at the side of the visionaries at Medugorje. Made precious because it has been with me through many hours of joy and sorrow, it is a constant companion, a sign of hope, a link with heaven, with heaven's Queen, our life, our sweetness, and our hope.

It is amazing, the role a humble string of beads has taken on for so many Christian peoples. Popes have repeatedly written encyclicals about it. The Queen of Heaven herself has brought it to earth in her apparitions, recommended its use, and even fingered it as her children said its prayers. Yet I have struggled with the rosary. And I know I am not alone in this. It comes to us so highly and powerfully recommended that to simply ignore it would be difficult. It has in fact been so powerfully present in my own life at times, and in the lives of those whom I have loved, that I could never set it aside. I have often prayed the rosary with a deep sense of satisfaction and consolation. There have been times when I could not conceive of letting a day go by without praying at least five (if not fifteen) decades. (A decade is a division of the rosary that consists primarily of ten Hail Marys.) At such times I would not have wanted to venture forth without the rosary in my pocket. And yet I have to admit that there have been other periods in my life when I have scarcely given the beads a thought—times when I would have been hard pressed to say exactly when the last time I prayed with them was. There have been times when I have worked my way through them sheerly out of a sense of duty and have experienced them as an obstacle rather than as a help in prayer.

That brings me to the reason that I am writing this book. There is an old saying: the best way to learn something is to teach it. I know the value of the rosary in my life; I know it from experience. Yet I know I have at times let it slip away. I want the reality of the rosary to so grasp me that I will never let it slip away again. I want to explore different ways of praying the rosary, not only to ward off boredom but to enable it to be a more powerful instrument of prayer in my life. And I want to share all of this with you, because I love you and I want your life also to be enriched by this precious reality. I know that in my effort to share my thoughts on the rosary, they will become clearer for me and become a more powerful presence in my life.

Fr. M. Basil

Feast of the Holy Rosary

PRAYING BY HAND

1

A Human Phenomenon: Beads Belong to Us All

Kalu Rimpoche sat with his back to the corner. His flowing robes fully concealed his body, but he seemed to be settled into the lotus position. Though he was not young, neither was he as old as the heavy lines in his face suggested. Rather than age, these lines bore witness to years of austerity lived in the cold, bleak mountains of Tibet. On his right sat one of his younger disciples, who translated the master's exalted language into the vernacular. To his left was a young Canadian, who then made the translation from Tibetan into English. This double translation could have made for a very tedious conversation. However, I seemed to know what the old man was saying long before the translated word completed its journey. And I believe that he experienced the same comprehension of what I was sharing with him. I was fascinated by this saintly refugee, who carried a living tradition with him, concerned to find someplace where it could be safely planted until it could return to its native Tibet.

During our whole conversation his lips never ceased moving, nor did his fingers. He had a most interesting string of beads. There were 100 saffron-colored beads and three pendants, each with ten movable beads. Each time he completed the large circle, he would move along a bead on the first pendant. When 1,000 mantras had been said and the ten beads on the first pendant had been moved along, he would move a bead on the second pendant. When these ten had been moved, he would then move a bead on the third. Thus he counted out 100,000 mantras, part of a continuous lifetime recitation of his sacred mantra.

Who first devised this ingenious string of bead, and when, are facts lost in the mists of the mountains and in the hallowed cells of the monasteries of ancient Tibet. Beads seem to belong to all peoples now, and to every religious tradition. One of the relics that Thomas Merton left behind, now enshrined in the chapel of his hermitage, is a string of saffron beads that he received in India not long before his death. They are elaborately carved, 108 in number. These particular beads were to be worn around the neck and used, as were Kalu's, to count mantras. The most ancient recorded use of prayer beads is found among the Hindus in India. They seem to have passed the practice on to the Buddhists in Tibet and China, who in turn passed it on to Japan. One hundred eight is a common number of beads, though in Burma the Buddhist monks have a string of seventy-two black beads made of rolled and lacquered petals that they call *buddhi*, "illumination."

Among the Muslims, a chaplet of ninety-nine beads, generally having a pendant with a special knot of richer material and a tassel, is used to recite the ninety-nine names of Allah, though sometimes the devout simply repeat the name Allah itself. Often there is added a special bead called the *iman*, or "leader," which stands for the "real," inexpressible name of God.

Beads are often wooden, though dried seeds of one kind or another are also common. Buddhists especially prize wood from the boddhi tree and Christians that from the olive—most especially from olive trees in the garden at Gethsemane. Glass of all colors has also been a favorite material. Strings of jewels or semiprecious stones are also favored, though they are usually the prerogative of higher castes, priests, or rulers. Some truly exquisite and priceless sets of beads were produced in the Middle Ages and worn as signs of high rank and great devotion. Knotted beads made from wool or hemp or similar substances do not survive well, so we have few examples of these from earlier times, although we think they were often used. Where the environment provided, shells were also strung and used like beads. In modern times artificial substances often provide the material for beads.

Just as the beads themselves vary, all sorts of materials have been used to string them together—precious and less so, more durable and less so. Sometimes a single strand of wool or hemp has served to create the beads and bond them together.

Although beads have been worn for purely ornamental purposes, they have also been given symbolic significance—especially when set in particular patterns—distinguishing the wearer or placing him under the protection of the divine. Beads have been worn around the neck, around the wrist, around the finger, and around the waist, as well as in headdresses and breastplates and in many other ways. And in all these ways, they have been used for spiritual and prayerful purposes.

Numbers have often been a part of the sacred heritage of peoples. To attain a sacred number or fulfill a certain commitment, beads are used to count sacred phrases or formulas. They also help to define the duration of one's prayer, though they are not wholly reliable in this; for as the pray-er enters more deeply into prayer, time can slip away. I can remember my mother wondering aloud why it took her so long to pray a rosary in her later years.

Fingering beads often helps our concentration. This is one of their greater benefits. While they occupy and integrate our external senses into our prayer, our mind is left freer to attend to its own level of reality. There are mysteries to be pondered and experiences to be had, moments of enlightenment and touches of the divine, while the beads and their accompanying formulas keep the lower faculties occupied. Even when the rational mind is occupied in conversation or some other simple task, beads can support the spirit in its course of prayer. Deliberately holding the beads can in itself be the prayer, especially when the mind seems unable to formulate any meaningful thoughts. The chain of beads can reach far beyond itself, bonding us with a higher power—with heaven itself. A lifetime of absorbed myth, rich legends, frequent use, and association with significant moments can endow a little chaplet with powerful symbolic meanings very personal to the hand and heart that hold it.

Our rosaries are very special to each one of us. Yet they belong to a great and rich human tradition. Realizing this can give our prayer not only a sense of solidarity with all the Christians who have gone before us fingering the beads but also a very profound ecumenical and interreligious meaning. May all of us who pray the beads and reach out to God, however we know him, one day come to know him as One and be one in him.

2

The Christian Rosary

Abba Paul sat cross-legged before his little cell. The sun was nearing the horizon, and the coolness of the desert night was beginning to seep in. There were two small piles of smooth, rounded stones on the ground before him. He quietly picked up a single stone from one pile and placed it on the other. He repeated this action again and again. All the while, his lips were moving. Abba Paul was saying his evening "rosary." While his fingers gently moved the stones and his lips repeated the familiar prayer his spiritual father had given him so long ago, his mind entered deeply into the divine. The stones enabled him to keep track of the prayer itself, not just the number of repetitions. While his fingers mechanically moved the stones and his lips repeated the words, his mind was able to rest undistracted within. It was only when the last stone had been moved that this father of the desert stirred from his evening prayer.

Who taught the holy old man this way of prayer? Perhaps it was the Spirit herself. Or perhaps his spiritual father, now long dead. But if the latter, whence had *he* learned it? We are in touch with a living tradition that may reach back to the Lord Jesus himself: "There are also many other things that Jesus did, but if these were to be described individually, I do not think the whole world would contain the books that would be written" (John 21:25, paraphrased).

The radical form of Christian living called *monasticism* found its way from the deserts of Egypt to wherever Christianity spread. It was carried by the fathers, but perhaps it also sprang up spontaneously under the movement of the Spirit. Mount Athos, the oldest republic in our world today, is a monastic republic. Saint Athanasius wrote the *typicon* (or basic constitution) for the Holy Mountain, as it is called, over 1,000 years ago. Although some of the early communities there have passed away and new ones have been founded and developed to take their place in the ruling assembly, the practices and customs of the monks have remained remarkably stable. Some have claimed that nothing has changed since the time of the seventh ecumenical council in 787, but there is evidence to the contrary.

I was very conscious of being immersed in age-old tradition during a wonderful long retreat I spent at Mount Athos. The *hegumen* of Simonos Petras, who was also the *gerontas* (or spiritual father) of the community, had an unusual practice. He marked the visit of special guests by calling one of his monks to profession and giving the newly professed the name of the visitor. When I arrived in darkness for the night office at the *katholikon* (the main chapel of the monastery) on the morning of my departure from the Holy Mountain, I was aware that something special was stirring the usual early-morning quiet. As the office progressed and we moved toward the eucharistic liturgy, the young monk who served as cook was led into the choir stripped of his usual robe. After many prostrations and prayers, he was gradually clothed with the monastic habit that had lain all the night on the altar in preparation. Finally he was given a cross, a lighted candle, a prayer cord, and a new name, Basil. The prayer cord was placed on his wrist, where it would stay virtually all the days of his life, always within easy reach whenever his hand was free from other occupations. It was there to encourage him in the constant prayer that was never to leave his lips. Only when he was buried would the cord be removed to be hung on the cross over his grave.

A few weeks before this I had stopped at the monastery of Zographou. While I ate the simple meal that Father Methodius had graciously prepared for me, I watched the quiet little man. He sat across the table from me busily making a prayer cord. He explained to me that each of the knots was actually woven of twenty-one knots, each with its own special meaning. In effect, the prayer was actually woven into the beads. The apparently simple cord, with its hundred knotted beads and woven cross, is full of symbolism. (Our Byzantine brothers and sisters are not happy when we impose the Western name of rosary on their prayer cord. The Greeks call it a *komvoschinion*; the Russians, a *tchotki*. We would perhaps do best to call it simply a prayer cord.) It is usually woven of black wool; however, the shops at the port of Mount Athos and elsewhere offer more elaborate cords, woven of different colors and even adorned with pompoms on the cross. Beads are used as well: sometimes a solid bead will mark off each twenty-five knots, or the whole might be made of strung beads. Everywhere in Greece men are found fingering small chaplets of beads, although (in a desacralized society) these are often referred to as "worry beads." I am sure that, as the owners fidget with them, the beads evoke a mute prayer somewhere deep within. I have never seen Greek women with these worry beads, but often a prayer cord is in their hands.

The prayer cord in the Eastern Christian tradition is used most often with the Jesus prayer: *Lord Jesus Christ, Son of the living God, have mercy on me a sinner*. This, too, came from the desert tradition. As the novice entered more and more deeply into the prayer it would tend to simplify itself until it became but one word: *Jesus*. The pray-er would enter into an ever deeper union with Jesus, until he or she was one with the Son to the Father in Holy Spirit. There has been an optional form allowing the introduction of a Marian phrase: *Lord Jesus Christ, Son of the living God, at the intercession of the most blessed God-Bearer, have mercy on me a sinner*. But this particular form has never become very widespread in its use.

Legend tells us that it was the Blessed Virgin Mary herself who gave Saint Dominic the rosary as we know it in the West, when she appeared to him during his labors to convert the Albigensian heretics. Although this legend was introduced into the life of Dominic some two centuries after his death (in a late-fifteenth-century life of Saint Dominic by Alan de la Roche), it nonetheless attests to the devotion of the Dominican family to the rosary and to its propagation among the peoples to whom they preach. It also attests to the fact that the rosary as we know it is the product of a gradual evolution.

It began as the layperson's psalter. The ancient psalter, or *Book of Psalms*, contains 150 inspired poems or songs. Saint Benedict of Nursia, who in the sixth century wrote the rule that largely governs the life of nuns and monks in the West, prescribed that his disciples should pray these 150 psalms at least once a week, noting that in earlier times more fervent monks did this each day. As novices, Benedict's disciples were expected to commit the psalms to memory, a special time being provided for this in the early morning. The prayer of the laity was inspired by and modeled on that of the monastery, which frequently stood in the midst of their town and to whose church they gathered for prayer. But the psalms were too complicated for many of the more simple, so a "psalter" of 150 *Paters* ("Our Fathers") was conceived, along with a string of beads to count them.

Besides the canonical office prescribed by the rule, most monasteries also celebrated a "little office" of the Blessed Virgin Mary each day. So it is not surprising that a "psalter of Mary" quickly found its place alongside that of the *Paters*. The *Paters* were replaced by the angelic salutation taken from the Gospel of Saint Luke: *Ave, Maria, gratia plena. Dominus tecum. Hail, Mary, full of grace. The Lord is with you.* In the twelfth century *Blessed are you among women, and blessed is the fruit of your womb* (1:42), also drawn from Luke's Gospel, began to be added to the *Ave*, or Hail Mary. The next century saw the addition of the holy name, Jesus. The second part of the Hail Mary (*Holy Mary, Mother of God, pray for us sinners now and at the hour of our death. Amen*) came into common usage only in the sixteenth century—the century during which the Doxology was first added at the end of each decade, just as the monks added it at the end of each psalm. Beginning in the thirteenth century, the string of beads was often reduced to fifty for morning, midday, and evening recitation, and these fifty were divided into tens by a bead called the *paternoster*, thus interspersing the Lord's Prayer among the *Aves*.

Thomas of Contimpre seems to be the first, around 1250, to call this a rosary—*rosarium*, a rose garden. Perhaps we most truly enter into the spirit of the rosary if we enter it as a rose garden, with its white roses of joy, its red roses of sorrow, and its golden-yellow roses of glory. There are thorns and the red of blood; but there is the joy of the garden throughout, for these are expressions of an immense love. The mysteries of the life, death, and resurrection of our Lord, Jesus Christ, and of his mother are the cause of our joy. The moments we spend with the rosary are moments spent in a garden of love.

When the monks and nuns recited or sang the psalms in choir, they often added to them certain antiphons. These short reflections, frequently drawn from Scripture, were inspired by the particular feast or liturgical season. This practice, too, in its own way was carried over into the psalter of the laity. One of the earliest collections of these rosary "antiphons" or scriptural reflections, commemorating the joys of Mary, is attributed to the Cistercian Saint Bernard of Clairvaux (✝ 1153). In the next century one of his Cistercian sons, Stephen of Salley, wrote more fully of the fifteen joyful mysteries. Series reflecting on Mary's sorrows and glories appeared later. At first it seems there was a phrase added to each *Ave* as there was an antiphon for each psalm. As the rosary came to be divided into decades, however—Henry Egher of Kolkar, the Carthusian (✝ 1408), is the first one to clearly set forth a rosary consisting of fifteen decades with a *Pater* and ten *Aves* in each—the antiphons or scriptural reflections came to be reduced to fifteen mysteries. Before the end of the fifteenth century, the fifteen we know today were universally popular. In 1483 a Dominican published a book entitled *Our Dear Lady's Psalter*. The fifteen mysteries he set forth are those we now have, except for the last two. The assumption and coronation of Mary are reflected upon during his fourteenth decade, and the fifteenth turns to the last judgment.

In the earliest historical apparitions of Mary, such as those at Guadalupe (1531) and later at Paris (1830), the rosary is not seen. At Lourdes Mary has a long rosary over her arm. When Bernadette begins to pray her rosary, Mary fingers her beads but does not move her lips. At Fatima in 1917 the rosary attains a special importance. Mary herself taught Jacinta how to pray the rosary properly. It was already a daily practice of the children to whom she chose to appear. An angel taught them to add to each decade of the rosary a particular prayer: *O Jesus, forgive us our sins, save us from the fires of hell. Lead all souls to heaven, especially those who are most in need of your mercy.* Mary called upon everyone to pray the rosary daily for peace on earth, and in particular for the conversion of Russia, which had at that time just embraced an atheistic communism. At the last apparition, just before the great miracle of the dancing sun, Mary declared, "I am the Lady of the Rosary. Let them continue to say the rosary every day." In an earlier appearance she had said, "Continue to say the five decades of the rosary every day in honor of Our Lady of the Rosary to obtain the peace of the world and the end of war."

In the apparitions that have been taking place in Medugorje, although Mary does not herself bear the rosary, she does encourage its use. On June 25, 1985, she said to the seers, "Dear Children, I ask you to ask everyone to pray the rosary. With the rosary you will overcome all the troubles Satan is trying to inflict on the Catholic Church. . . . Let all the priests pray the rosary. Give time to the rosary." The apparitions usually take place while the community is praying this prayer. Mary is insistent at Medugorje on prayer in the heart; words are not enough.

"Private" apparitions such as these do not pertain to the formal revelation or teaching of the Church. At most, the local bishops might examine them and declare that they are worthy of credence. The popes and bishops of recent years have given singular recognition to the apparitions at both Lourdes and Fatima, however.

Recognition of the rosary itself came much earlier. The bull *Ea Quae* (May 12, 1479) of Pope Sixtus IV was the first dedicated to the rosary. It extolled this form of prayer as a means to grow in faith. He saw it also as a powerful weapon against the enemies of the Church. Pope Saint Pius V saw it the same way when he attributed to the "arms" of the rosary the naval victory at Lepanto (October 7, 1571), which prevented the Islamic invasion of Europe. He established October 7 as the Feast of the Most Holy Rosary, to be celebrated throughout the whole Church. His bull *Consueverunt Romani Pontifices* recognized the form of the rosary as it had developed, and he canonized it, as it were: ". . . the veneration of the Blessed Virgin Mary through the repetition of the angelic salutation one hundred and fifty times, according to the number of the Psalms of David, interrupting each decade with an Our Father and some specific meditations which illustrate the whole life of Our Lord Jesus Christ."

Through the succeeding centuries pope after pope honored the rosary and encouraged its use with their pens and with their voices in their addresses to the faithful. Most outstanding is Pope Leo XIII. This Holy Father came to the throne late in life, at the end of the nineteenth century, but he had nonetheless a long reign. In the course of it he published fifteen encyclicals in honor of the rosary, creating what we might call his own particular rosary.

Another holy person is creating her own special rosary in our own time. A friend of mine who spent a month with Mother Teresa in Calcutta wrote, "She already has five houses open in Russia and another five ready to open—she calls them the five joyful and five sorrowful mysteries—and she wants five more houses—the glorious mysteries—to open there as well." When the recitation of the rosary bears this kind of fruit, we know that it is a powerful prayer indeed. For as our Lord has said, we can judge a tree by its fruit (Matt. 12:33).

In the course of the evolution of the rosary as it is most commonly practiced, other forms also evolved. Some of them have continued in use to our times. One of the more ancient of these is the Bridgettine rosary, which is proper to the daughters of Saint Bridget of Sweden, the nuns of the Order of the Most Holy Savior. This rosary has six decades, each made up of a *Pater*, ten *Aves*, and the Apostles' Creed. At the end of the six decades, a *Pater* and three *Aves* are recited. The sixty-three *Aves* honor the sixty-three years of our Lady's life—her age at death, according to Saint Bridget. The seven *Paters* commemorate the seven joys and seven sorrows our Lord's life brought to Mary.

The Servites continue to propagate a rosary in honor of the seven sorrows of the Blessed Virgin Mary. The idea of entering into Mary's sorrows is very ancient in Christian practice. In the fourth century Abba Poeman, a father of the desert, spoke of his experience: "My mind was there with Blessed Mary, the Mother of God, who was weeping over the cross of the Savior. I too would weep with her always." Meditation on the sorrowful mysteries of the rosary, and even the joyful (Simeon's prophecy at the presentation, and the loss of Jesus before the finding in the fifth joyful mystery), invite such compassion. Devotion to the sorrows of Mary received special impetus in the fourteenth century, marked as it was by the sorrows of the Black Death. In the course of the next century the seven sorrows were well established and a seven-decade rosary had come into common use. The seven sorrows commonly enumerated are these:

The prophecy of Simeon (Luke 2:34–35)

The flight into Egypt (Matt. 2:13–21)

The loss of Jesus for three days (Luke 2:41–50)

The ascent to Calvary (John 19:17)

The crucifixion (John 19:18–30)

Jesus taken down from the cross (John 19:39–40)

The burial of Jesus (John 19:40–42)

ꑄ

In 1422 the Franciscans introduced a seven-decade rosary that came to be called the Franciscan Crown. It is used to commemorate the seven joys of Mary: the annunciation, the visitation, the nativity of our Lord, the adoration of the Magi, the finding of young Jesus in the temple, the apparition of the risen Christ to his mother, and the assumption and coronation of the Blessed Virgin in heaven. The crown originally consisted of seven Our Fathers and seventy Hail Marys. Later two more Hail Marys were added, because it was believed in this tradition that Mary lived to be seventy-two. The Franciscans also added an Our Father, a Hail Mary, and a Doxology for the intentions of the pope.

3

The Prayers of the Rosary

As we have seen, the rosary is a method of prayer or meditation that developed within the Christian community over the course of centuries. It contains certain elements that are very basically human and are therefore common to all traditions of spirituality. At the same time, the rosary is a uniquely Christian prayer, coming forth under the guidance of the Holy Spirit from the faith and love of the Christian community to express and nurture that faith and love.

We have spoken at length about the beads themselves. Now let us look at the prayers that accompany them.

The Sign of the Cross

In the name of the Father and of the Son and of the Holy Spirit. Amen.

Christianity is a religion of incarnation. Our central dogma is that of the incarnation of One of the Three. We believe that every person is an incarnate spirit who will live forever. Our prayer is most properly ours when it is incarnate, made up of bodily actions and words as well as of thoughts and aspirations of the heart—of faith, hope, and love.

We begin the rosary with a bodily gesture and words, with an act of faith and love. This signals that it is time for prayer. We sign our body with the life-giving cross, renewing the consecration of our baptism. As our hand goes from forehead to breast, from left shoulder to right, we acknowledge that we are wholly the Lord's and have been wholly saved by the Lord's saving cross. We acknowledge, too, that we are a temple of the Holy Trinity. As Jesus promised at the Last Supper, he and the Father have taken up their dwelling within us. The Holy Spirit, too, is within, to teach us all things, bringing to mind all that Jesus has taught us. We consecrate the prayer we are about to make wholly to God-Triune. We pray in their name, and not just by some extrinsic delegation. We acknowledge that we have been baptized into Christ, brought into the inner life of the Trinity; that we have in some way been divinized, made partakers of the divine life and nature.

In our beginning we have our end. For all prayer has but one end, ultimately: that all be brought fully into unity in Christ to the glory of the Father in the Holy Spirit.

Usually as we make the sign of the cross, we hold in our hand the crucifix that hangs at the end of the pendant of our rosary. Touching to ourselves this cross with the image of the dying Christ, we further acknowledge that we are consecrated by his life-giving death and that all that we do is made worthy and efficacious by that same saving love. We kiss the cross as an expression of our gratitude and love. And then we continue our prayer.

The Apostles' Creed

I believe in God, the Father almighty, creator of heaven and earth, and in Jesus Christ, his only Son, our Lord, who was conceived by the Holy Spirit, born of the Virgin Mary, suffered under Pontius Pilate, was crucified, died, and was buried. He descended into hell. The third day he rose again from the dead. He ascended into heaven and sits at the right hand of the Father. From thence he shall come to judge the living and the dead. I believe in the Holy Spirit, the holy catholic Church, the communion of saints, the forgiveness of sins, the resurrection of the body, and life everlasting. Amen.

The Apostles' Creed is one of the oldest creedal formulas we have. It was probably not composed by the Twelve themselves, as some legends would have it, but it touches upon apostolic times. In the Creed we express our faith in what we will be meditating upon as we pray the rosary. *Fides quaerens intellectum* is a very ancient formula: faith seeking understanding. We profess our faith and in our prayer seek to understand it more fully, not only with the mind but also with the heart, so that it will be a living faith expressing itself in action.

Again, we begin with the end: God the Father, the creator. All has come forth from him. In some mysterious way he generates the Son and sends him forth so that all might return to the Father in the loving Kiss who is the Holy Spirit. We believe in God, the Father almighty, creator of heaven and earth. And in Jesus Christ, his Son, our Lord: the incarnation, the birth, the passion and death, the resurrection and ascension—all the mysteries we will be rehearsing as we move through the decades.

We believe in the Holy Spirit, the Lord, *Kyrios*, who, like Jesus, is true God of true God. The life-giving Spirit who has become our spirit in baptism, who dwells within us to teach us all. It is she who gives life to our faith, to our prayer, to our rosary.

We believe in the catholic Church, the universal Church. It is with this Church, which is spread throughout the universe and of which we are members, that we now pray. We believe in the communion of saints. Yes, this Church does extend throughout the universe and beyond. And we pray now with all the members, those on earth and those in heaven. We pray with every saint who ever held the beads in his or her hands—including that sainted grandmother who first taught me how to pray this rosary. We pray even with the glorious Queen of Heaven,

Queen of the Rosary (even as we pray *to* her), who—as at Lourdes—passes the beads through her fingers, endorsing our prayer.

And as we pray, we believe in the fruit of our prayer. We believe in that fullness of the forgiveness of sins that includes freedom from the effects of sin—death and the grave; it includes the resurrection of the body and life everlasting. As we enter into our prayer, life everlasting is already begun for us. Amen.

Our Father: The Pater

Our Father, who art in heaven, hallowed be thy name. Thy kingdom come. Thy will be done on earth as it is in heaven. Give us this day our daily bread. And forgive us our trespasses as we forgive those who trespass against us. Lead us not into temptation, but deliver us from evil.

Saints have written books on the Our Father. When Jesus gave his disciples this prayer, he did not give us a formula to be rattled off. Rather, he gave us a whole school of prayer—a prayer that sums up all the attitudes that should guide us, forming in us the mind and heart of Christ. I will not, therefore, attempt here a commentary on this pregnant prayer. Instead, I leave it to your meditations made fruitful by the inspirations of the indwelling Spirit.

I would, however, like to share one thought. Today there is a new realization of how male-dominated our outlook in every area of life during the last few thousand years has been. In light of this realization, we are beginning to appreciate more what are called the *feminine* or *maternal* qualities of God as they are revealed to us in the sacred Scriptures. This is very good. However, I would not like to see the fatherly role of God in our lives in any way watered down or lost. I think perhaps our need for this role is even greater today than it has been in the past: we face what has been aptly but sadly called a generation without fathers. The absence of a fatherly presence in the life of so many makes it all the more needful that God's fatherly goodness and care, his rich "masculine" qualities, come to play more powerfully in the lives of his children. When God brings us into a participation in his own divinity through the adoptive and transforming graces of baptism, he does not want us to be any less human. He has provided for us both a heavenly father and a heavenly mother—one divine, the other human. In the rosary we can learn to let Mary fulfill in our lives that role which has been hers since Calvary ("Behold thy mother") and also learn to let God the Father fulfill the role in our lives that he fulfilled in the life of the most perfect and perfectly fulfilled human who ever walked this earth and who constantly looked to him as Father. Jesus in his teaching was playing into the outlook of his time and place. There is room, and always has been, for development of understanding and insight into what he has taught us. Our understanding of God can indeed be enriched by a fuller appreciation of her "feminine" attributes. Every male can understand himself more fully and function more satisfyingly and authentically if he is open to his feminine side. So let the masculine be strengthened by an integration of the feminine. Let God's fatherly attributes play an ever stronger role in our lives, even as her feminine attributes begin to have their impact. Jesus is our model. For him, God was father and Mary mother, although Joseph had a fatherly role to play and the Father's motherly qualities, breathing through the Spirit, also had a role. We can expose ourselves regularly to these realities under the Spirit's gentle, powerful leading as we pray our daily rosary. *Our Father . . . Holy Mary, Mother . . .*

The origins of the Our Father are very clear and simple. Saint Matthew's Gospel has Jesus himself teach us the prayer. Thus the prayer readily found its place at the center of Christian prayer from the beginning. It is not surprising that it made its way into Mary's psalter.

Hail Mary: The Ave

Hail, Mary, full of grace. The Lord is with you. Blessed are you among women, and blessed is the fruit of your womb, Jesus. Holy Mary, Mother of God, pray for us sinners now and at the hour of our death. Amen.

The *Ave* also has a gospel origin, though not entirely. It was not offered there as a prayer, and the form we know only gradually came together. The earliest rosary or psalter of Mary was made up of the earliest form of the *Ave*—simply the angelic salutation: "Hail, Mary, full of grace. The Lord is with you." In the little office of the Blessed Virgin Mary, as it was recited in the monastic choirs, the antiphonal response to this angelic salutation was the greeting that Elizabeth gave to her cousin: "Blessed are you among women, and blessed is the fruit of your womb." The carryover to the psalter of our Lady was quite natural.

Pope Urban IV (1261–1264) asked the faithful to add "Jesus Christ." In the course of the following centuries, however, the title "Christ" got lost. Perhaps it was because one of the earlier popular forms of the rosary added a different modifying phrase after each repetition of the *Ave* (Jesus, born of Mary; Jesus, risen from the dead; and so on), and the inclusion of the Christ title proved too cumbersome.

Up to this point, the *Ave* is not a prayer in the sense of a petition. It is simply an honorific salutation. Phrases from the offices of the monks, such as "Pray for us, O holy Mother of God," led to further additions to the *Ave*. Various phrases were used until "Holy Mary, Mother of God, pray for us sinners now and at the hour of our death" became common by the end of the fifteenth century. Pope Saint Pius V canonized this wording in his breviary of 1568.

It would be hard to doubt the presence of the Holy Spirit guiding this long evolution, for the result is an exquisitely beautiful prayer. With one of heaven's great spirits as our mentor, we approach Mary with gracious delicacy, honoring her greatest prerogatives: that she is totally pleasing to God, filled with God, worthy to be the mother of God. We honor her for what she is:

woman. And we delight her in honoring her child, calling him blessed. Graciousness opens the way for grace. We can now make our petition. We pray to the mother of God, knowing that nothing can be denied her. (Remember Cana.) She, as a mother, knows our needs far better than we, so we content ourselves simply to ask her intercession for us now, caring for our present needs, and at that hour when we will experience our greatest need and most want a mother near. It is not surprising to me how often a Christian who has used the rosary through life holds it in his or her hand at the hour of death—a witness of faith, a pledge of heaven, a silent but powerful prayer.

Glory Be to the Father: The Gloria

Glory be to the Father and to the Son and to the Holy Spirit, as it was in the beginning, is now, and ever shall be, world without end. Amen.

The *Gloria*, or "little Doxology," is an ancient prayer. Already in the third century the monks added it to each psalm and to the responsories they sang after the lessons at the office. It was a time when the Church was entering into the struggle for an adequate expression of the mystery of the three persons in the one God. *Lex orandi lex credendi*: the law of prayer is the law of faith. The constant adoration of the Three as one God by the faithful guided the Church through the centuries of theological debate to a clear definition.

In the early twelfth century the Cistercian laybrothers were given an office of *Paters*, with each followed by a *Gloria*, although no *Glorias* were added to their little office of *Aves*. The *Glorias* came to be added to the decades of the rosary itself only three centuries later, when the Dominicans began to chant it in choir. It certainly is fitting and desirable that our thoughts on each of the mysteries and our prayers should culminate in the Holy Trinity. For this is the reality. All that Jesus and Mary lived was to the glory of the Trinity and was to bring us, one with the Son, into the inner life of the Trinity—the life of total gift of self in love.

The Fatima Prayer

O Jesus, forgive us our sins, save us from the fires of hell. Lead all souls to heaven, especially those who are most in need of your mercy.

The Fatima Prayer is the latest addition to the rosary. In 1917 the Lady of the Rosary appeared repeatedly to three children at Fatima. She spoke often of hell and taught the children to add this little prayer at the end of each decade of the rosary. Because of the emphasis on the daily rosary in the Fatima revelations and the high degree of credence these apparitions have received within the Church, this prayer has come into almost universal usage.

The memory that usually remains most vividly with people visiting a Cistercian abbey is that of the evening *Salve*. The sun has set and the monks have gathered in the church. In the dark they chant the familiar psalms of Compline, which brings the monastic day to a close. As the abbot pronounces the final bless-ing, the image of our Lady above the high altar is illuminated. The monks stand out of their choir stalls in ceremony. Then the profoundly beautiful chant that century after century has com-pleted the monks' day of worship and prayer fills the abbey church with its plaintive tones and lifts every eye and heart to Mary.

Hail, Holy Queen: The Salve Regina

Hail, holy Queen, Mother of Mercy, our life, our sweetness, and our hope. To you do we cry, poor banished children of Eve. To you do we send up our sighs, mourning and weeping in this valley of tears. Turn, then, most gracious Advocate, your eyes of mercy toward us. And after this our exile show unto us the blessed Fruit of your womb, Jesus. O clement, O loving, O sweet Virgin Mary.

The *Salve Regina* was written in the ninth century by a monk named Herman and quickly became the favorite evening song of monks everywhere. As the story has it, originally the *Salve* did not include the final three O's. Then one night in the cathedral of Speyer, after all the people had ended their singing, Bernard of Clairvaux, who had been drawn up into ecstacy, went on: "O clement, O loving, O sweet Virgin Mary."

It is easy to see how the monks' practice of ending their day of psalm-singing with the *Salve* led to its being adopted for the conclusion of the rosary. The words alone convey the plaintiveness of one who has had a long, laborious day and is ready to retire. He is ready to retire from this land of exile and go home to the eternal rest. Through the long day of exile, the Queen of Heaven, who is mercy herself, a source or mother of mercy, has been a sweet presence, a source of ongoing hope. This hymn is but the cry of a weary heart to a mother who understands.

Often the *Salve* is followed by a versicle and response taken from the little office of the Blessed Virgin and the prayer from the Mass of the Feast of the Holy Rosary.

> *Pray for us, O Holy Mother of God.*
> *That we may be made worthy of the promises of Christ.*
>
> *Let us pray: Pour forth, we beseech you, O Lord, your grace into our hearts, that we to whom the incarnation of Christ your Son was made known by the message of an angel may by his passion and cross be brought to the glory of his resurrection, through the same Christ, our Lord. Amen.*

4

Praying the Rosary

The rosary is a method, an instrument, of prayer. It was given to us by God through the Church to help us to pray, to enter into communion and union with God. Therefore, we should feel free to use it or pray it in any way that helps us to enter into that union.

Of the many ways in which the rosary can be prayed, no one is *a priori* better than the others. Using one rather than another does not mark a certain progress in prayer. On a particular day or at a particular time of the day, for one reason or another, one approach to praying the beads might better suit us or be more attractive to us. In the weariness of the evening, I might be more comfortable with a quieter, more contemplative rosary; in the morning something more active and engaging might better serve me. Remember always: prayer is the thing. Communion with God is what we are about, what we are interested in—not saying the rosary well or in the most "advanced" way. *We want to pray.*

The three ways discussed here of praying the rosary—the literal, the meditative, and the contemplative—are only suggestions, opening out into a limitless number of variations. They come from lived experience and have known many, many variations in my own continued effort to pray the rosary.

In the *literal* approach, we simply pray the prayers of the rosary: the Our Father, the Hail Mary, and the Doxology, as well as the Sign of the Cross, the Creed, and the Hail Holy Queen. (I guess I almost always pray this last prayer in a quite literal way.)

There is a lot of variety in these few prayers. In fact, all the forms of prayer are represented: the serious, suppliant attitude of the Our Father, the joyful, lyrical praise of the Hail Mary, the profound, contemplative adoration of the Doxology, all grounded on the faith of the Creed. While our lips and mind dwell upon the words and attitudes of these prayer formulas, deep within our spirit there is a communing with God that allows the Holy Spirit to pray within us as only she can. The deeper meanings of the words that we recite reveal themselves to us. We discover the richness of the prayer that Jesus taught us. We know something of Elizabeth's joy. We know that death is a part of life. We know what it is to adore.

Some days, when our minds are buffeted about by powerful currents, this concentration on the literal words we are saying with our lips seems to be the only way that we can enter into and remain in prayer, escaping the tyranny of our own thoughts and emotions. And literal prayer is good prayer. By the time we have persevered through the five decades, a peace has often taken hold of us. The emotions have abated; we are again masters of our own processes and able to face the crises of life with a certain serenity.

In the *meditative* approach, which can easily be combined with this literal approach, the pray-er pauses after the announcement of each mystery or after the Our Father for a time of meditation. This works well when a group is praying the rosary together, whether or not the individuals go on to pray the Hail Marys using the literal approach. The leader can announce the mystery and perhaps share some of his personal reflections on it. If the group is not too large, other members can be invited to add their own reflections aloud, enriching the experience for all.

I recall having dinner in the home of a wealthy Catholic family one evening. As we were finishing dessert, the youngest son, Chris, went over to the sideboard and brought to the table what looked like a large cigar box. When he opened it, I saw that the compartments were filled with rosaries. He circled the table and each person took a rosary. Then Maureen, age ten (it was her turn), started us off on a meditation on the second joyful mystery. After her initial sharing, we all joined in. We shared for quite a while (there are nine children in the family), followed by quiet. Then Maureen led us in the prayers of the decade. These family members, who had made the family rosary a part of their life for many, many years, were content to pray only a decade—but in a way that enabled them to enter more deeply into it.

We should not be afraid to try different approaches to make the rosary a more effective instrument of prayer in our lives. One aspect of the meditative approach is the *scriptural rosary*. Popular today, it harks back to a very early way of praying the rosary. Before each Hail Mary a phrase from sacred Scripture is interjected—one that refers to or throws light on the mystery being meditated upon during the decade. This somewhat complicated method was earlier abandoned because it required an exceptionally good memory, but today booklets with the texts for each bead are available. Such a way of praying the rosary has to be done very slowly, however, or it will be just a lot of words rather than a deeper entering into the mysteries.

Most of us, most of the time, will probably find ourselves letting go of the literal meaning of the prayers we are saying with our lips in order to concentrate on the mystery of the respective decade. There are many ways in which we can meditate on the mysteries of the rosary.

We can use our imagination to call up the gospel scene we are concerned about. In doing this we might remain external spectators, watching the scene unfold as it once did in history. Or we might enter into the scene and be a spectator or participant. There is no reason why one day we might not be an angel who has the privilege of witnessing the birth at Bethlehem as part of the heavenly choir, then singing of it and perhaps hastening (flying?) to nearby fields to bring tidings to shepherds. The next day we might be one of the shepherds who has hurried to the cave. We might be one of the animals who live in the cave and welcome the guests, or a little lamb brought as a gift. Or, if we dare, we might be Joseph or Mary or even the Child himself, letting the various emotions of our particular perspective well up in our hearts.

As we do this, we might be content to let the reality seep more and more deeply into us, calling forth whatever response it wills: adoration, wonderment, fear, love, repentance, hope, and so on. Or we might look to the mystery to see what particular virtue it calls for in our lives or inspires us to practice with more fidelity. Some authors have associated in their writings a particular virtue with each decade. I would rather not do that. I would rather leave the space open to the Spirit. On different occasions the same gospel reality can inspire us in different ways, depending in part on just where we are on our particular journey in faith.

Some days our meditation of each particular mystery may be virtually thoughtless. We are before the mystery, or it is before us, and we remain in silent openness. A deeper communion is being woven. A deeper molding of our spirit is taking place. Words, articulated thoughts, are neither sufficient nor necessary. They would only get in the way, distracting us from the reality that is operative here and now.

Other days our meditation might be primarily one of mental exploration, with little imaging. Questions about the mystery come to our mind, or we consider application of the mystery to our lives or to the problems we are presently grappling with. Those of us who like to think and explore ideas have to be careful that we do not reduce the rosary to speculations that have no connection with the heart. Mental prayer is prayer only when the operations of our mind, including those of our intellect, are geared to prayer, to union and communion with God. Again, the rosary is an instrument, a method, of *prayer*.

There will be days when *all* words and images and ideas get in the way. Yet because the rosary is precious to us, we do not want to abandon it. When going through the words or trying to imagine scenes seems only to take us away from God, it is best to move with the grace of the moment. It is time for a more completely *contemplative* approach to the rosary. It is enough simply to hold the rosary in our hands and be with God—perhaps within a particular mystery, perhaps not. Is this still "saying the rosary"? There are those who would argue that it is not, and maybe they are right. Is it even "*praying* the rosary"? What matter? Prayer is the thing. We do not want to be afraid to leave the instrument behind when it is no longer needed.

Let me add a little word of caution here. We must be careful not to let an overeagerness for contemplation or some misguided desire to "get ahead" in prayer move us to abandon the full use of this precious school of prayer. A gentle docility to the movement of the Spirit each day as we sit with our rosary is what must guide us in our approach to praying the beads—not some preconceived ideas.

Simply held silently in our hands, the rosary can still be for us very much an instrument of prayer. Indeed, this is probably the way we will say our last rosary and in some way keep on praying it even as we lie in our coffin. The silent grip says something about our bond with heaven, with Mary, and with the praying Church in its living tradition of prayer. As the Spirit prays within us, our incarnate body still has its part. A sacramental is still present as an outward sign of inner realities.

The important thing is that we make time in our all-too-busy days to sit with the rosary. Whether it be at home or in church, on the subway or walking down the street, we need a time when we let other things go and, with the help of this instrument, enter into prayer with Mary and the Church. We need to be in a prayer that has a certain spaciousness about it, be in a rose garden, letting the fragrance of the different mysteries of our salvation fill our spirit to enliven our faith and hope and love—in short, to refresh our spirit.

5

The Rosary and the Scriptures

The rosary is a gospel prayer. The orderly and gradual unfolding of the mysteries of the rosary makes present the way in which the Word of God, entering into our human journey, brought about our redemption. The mysteries take us through the principle salvific events accomplished by Christ, from his virginal conception and the mysteries of his childhood to the culminating moments of his Passover, his passion, and his glorious resurrection, and to the effects of these on the infant Church with the pentecostal outpouring of the Holy Spirit and the assumption and coronation of Mary, the mother of the Church. The division of the mysteries of the rosary into three parts not only adheres to the chronological order of events but also reflects the plan of the original proclamation of the faith and sets forth the mystery of Christ in the way in which it is seen by Saint Paul in his beautiful hymn in Philippians: kenosis, death, and exaltation (Phil. 2:6–11).

This method of prayer, then, is deeply concerned with the Scriptures. It builds up our faith by letting them speak to us: "Faith comes through hearing." It invites us to enter ever more deeply into them, letting them form our minds and our hearts until we have in us the mind that was in Christ Jesus.

We Christians believe that the sacred Scriptures, as they have been handed down to us through the centuries within the Church, were written under the direct inspiration of the Holy Spirit for our guidance and enlightenment. The Holy Spirit guides anyone who writes in faith, of course; it is only by grace that we can do such a thing. But we believe that the chosen texts that the Church has discerned to be part of the sacred Scriptures were inspired in a special way: God intended to use them consistently through the centuries as a means of speaking to his people. So when we approach the Scriptures, our attitude should be one of listening. God is speaking to us here and now through these words.

We know that when friends speak to us, the message that their words and concepts bear is greatly modified by the circumstances in which they speak. When God speaks to us through the Scriptures, he speaks to us here and now, where we are on our journey, where we are in our relationship with him. Thus the very same text can bring to us a different message from day to day. We need to really listen, to be attuned. When we are, we never tire of listening to the Scriptures—even to the same familiar texts—for their message is ever new, a message for here and now, for this moment on the journey. And always it is a message of love, even when it is a severe warning or a paternal correction.

Traditionally, the Church fathers and Christian exegetes are accustomed to speak of the various "senses" of Scripture, the various levels of meaning. There is the literal or historical sense—the straight-on meaning, the facts as they are related. This meaning is usually quite clear and often somewhat prosaic. For example, when Jesus was twelve, Mary and Joseph took him up to the Temple for the feast. Simple facts.

Yet even this literal sense can lead us into wonder and have a powerful message for us as we reflect on it: Who is this who is being "taken" up to the Temple? The very Son of God become man. God as a youth being led by two of his creatures. What awesome condescension; what humility! And *we* find it difficult to bend our proud necks to the leading of the hierarchs God sets over us even when he has promised to guide them so that they do not lead us astray. (And so on.)

There is much that we can draw from the literal sense of the Scriptures, especially as our imagination fruitfully makes its contribution. But if we restrict ourselves to the literal sense of Scripture, we close off from ourselves broad channels through which the Holy Spirit wants to communicate with us. Inspired by the Scriptures themselves—most notably, Saint Paul's Epistles—the fathers rightly discerned that beneath the literal sense there are hidden spiritual or mystical senses. Paul tells us that Sarah and Hagar are not only two women; they are two divinely ordered dispensations. He tells us that the rock that followed the wandering Israelites through the desert was not only a rock that gave them water; it was Christ.

As we meditate on the mysteries of the rosary, we do not want always to stop at a consideration of the literal sense or the historical scene. Our meditation and our lives will be enriched if we allow the deeper mystical sense to speak to us.

The fathers have focused on three kinds of spiritual senses. There is the *allegorical* sense, which reveals a deeper message (as when the story of Sarah is the story not only of a woman but also of the establishment of a dispensation of grace). There is also the *moral* sense, the call of the Scriptures to us to respond in a certain way to the divine dispensation. And finally there is the *anagogical* sense—a presaging of ultimate meaning, the consummation toward which all is directed.

Thus, for example, as we see Mary carry the little Child into the temple to present him to the Lord, mystically we see the Church bringing to God the Father the most perfect sacrifice of his own Son. We see Mary as mother and mediatrix, Mary as Church, bringing us to the Father in and with Christ. The moral meaning of this is to let ourselves be offered, to enter into the offering and let ourselves be fully purified in the offering of Christ. The consummation, of course, is when in fact Mary and Church have brought the whole Christ into the heavenly temple and all is pure and reconciled and we, like old Simeon, really *see*.

I am sure that you can already perceive that at the level of the spiritual sense there is no limit to what the Lord might say to us. Each day as we come to the rosary, we can with expectation open ourselves to the Word of God and let it speak to us. It would not hurt—indeed, it could be most helpful, if we have the time—to listen again to the pertinent passages of Scripture as we begin each decade. In time, of course, they will become (if they are not already) completely familiar to us, and the simple announcement of the mystery will bring them fully to mind. A quiet savoring of them will always be fruitful and inspiring.

In order to facilitate this, we include here the most pertinent passages of the Scriptures for each of the familiar fifteen mysteries.

The Annunciation

In the sixth month the angel Gabriel was sent by God to a town in Galilee called Nazareth, to a virgin betrothed to a man named Joseph, of the House of David; and the virgin's name was Mary. He went in and said to her, "Rejoice, you who enjoy God's favor! The Lord is with you." She was deeply disturbed by these words and asked herself what this greeting could mean, but the angel said to her, "Mary, do not be afraid; you have won God's favor. Look! You are to conceive in your womb and bear a son, and you must name him Jesus. He will be great and will be called Son of the Most High. The Lord God will give him the throne of his ancestor David; he will rule over the House of Jacob for ever and his reign will have no end." Mary said to the angel, "But how can this come about, since I have no knowledge of man?" The angel answered, "The Holy Spirit will come upon you, and the power of the Most High will cover you with its shadow. And so the child will be holy and will be called Son of God. And I tell you this too: your cousin Elizabeth also, in her old age, has conceived a son, and she whom people called barren is now in her sixth month, for nothing is impossible to God." Mary said, "You see before you the Lord's servant, let it happen to me as you have said." And the angel left her.

—Luke 1:26–38

The Visitation

Mary set out at that time and went as quickly as she could into the hill country to a town in Judah. She went into Zechariah's house and greeted Elizabeth. Now it happened that as soon as Elizabeth heard Mary's greeting, the child leapt in her womb and Elizabeth was filled with the Holy Spirit. She gave a loud cry and said, "Of all women you are the most blessed, and blessed is the fruit of your womb. Why should I be honored with a visit from the mother of my Lord? Look, the moment your greeting reached my ears, the child in my womb leapt for joy. Yes, blessed is she who believed that the promise made her by the Lord would be fulfilled."

And Mary said:

> My soul proclaims the greatness of the Lord
> and my spirit rejoices in God my Savior;
> because he has looked upon the humiliation of his
>   servant.
> Yes, from now onwards all generations will call me
>   blessed,
> for the Almighty has done great things for me.
> Holy is his name,
> and his faithful love extends age after age to those
>   who fear him.
> He has used the power of his arm,
> he has routed the arrogant of heart.
> He has pulled down princes from their thrones and
>   raised high the lowly.
> He has filled the starving with good things, sent
>   the rich away empty.

He has come to the help of Israel his servant,
   mindful of his faithful love—
according to the promise he made to our
   ancestors—
of his mercy to Abraham and to his descendants for
   ever.

Mary stayed with her some three months and then went home.

—Luke 1:39–56

The Birth of Jesus

Now it happened that at this time Caesar Augustus issued a decree that a census should be made of the whole inhabited world. This census—the first—took place while Quirinius was governor of Syria, and everyone went to be registered, each to his own town. So Joseph set out from the town of Nazareth in Galilee for Judaea, to David's town called Bethlehem, since he was of David's House and line, in order to be registered together with Mary, his betrothed, who was with child. Now it happened that, while they were there, the time came for her to have her child, and she gave birth to a son, her first-born. She wrapped him in swaddling clothes and laid him in a manger because there was no room for them in the living-space. In the countryside close by there were shepherds out in the fields keeping guard over their sheep during the watches of the night. An angel of the Lord stood over them and the glory of the Lord shone round them. They were terrified, but the angel said, "Do not be afraid. Look, I bring you news of great joy, a joy to be shared by the whole people. Today in the town of David a Savior has been born to you; he is Christ the Lord. And here is a sign for you: you will find a baby wrapped in swaddling clothes and lying in a manger. And all at once with the angel there was a great throng of the hosts of heaven, praising God with the words:

> Glory to God in the highest heaven,
> and on earth peace for those he favors.

Now it happened that when the angels had gone from them into heaven, the shepherds said to one another, "Let us go to Bethlehem and see this event which the Lord has made known to us." So they hurried away and found Mary and Joseph, and the baby lying in the manger. When they saw the child they repeated what they had been told about him, and everyone who heard it was astonished at what the shepherds said to them. As for Mary, she treasured all these things and pondered them in her heart. And the shepherds went back glorifying and praising God for all they had heard and seen, just as they had been told.

—Luke 2:1–20

The Presentation of Jesus in the Temple

And when the day came for [Jesus and Mary] to be purified in
keeping with the Law of Moses, [Mary and Joseph] took him
up to Jerusalem to present him to the Lord—observing what is
written in the Law of the Lord: Every first-born male must be
consecrated to the Lord—and also to offer in sacrifice, in ac-
cordance with what is prescribed in the Law of the Lord, a pair
of turtledoves or two young pigeons. Now in Jerusalem there
was a man named Simeon. He was an upright and devout man;
he looked forward to the restoration of Israel and the Holy
Spirit rested on him. It had been revealed to him by the Holy
Spirit that he would not see death until he had set eyes on the
Christ of the Lord. Prompted by the Spirit he came to the
Temple; and when the parents brought in the child Jesus to do
for him what the Law required, he took him into his arms and
blessed God and he said:

> Now, Master, you are letting your servant go in
>   peace as you promised;
> for my eyes have seen the salvation
> which you have made ready in the sight of the na-
>   tions;
> a light of revelation for the gentiles
> and glory for your people Israel.

As the child's father and mother were wondering at the things
that were being said about him, Simeon blessed them and said
to Mary his mother, "Look, he is destined for the fall and the
rise of many in Israel, destined to be a sign that is opposed—and
a sword will pierce your soul too—so that the secret thoughts
of many may be laid bare."

There was a prophetess, too, Anna the daughter of Phanuel, of the tribe of Asher. She was well on in years. Her days of girlhood over, she had been married for seven years before becoming a widow. She was now eighty-four years old and never left the Temple, serving God night and day with fasting and prayer. She came up just at that moment and began to praise God; and she spoke of the child to all who looked forward to the deliverance of Jerusalem.

—Luke 2:22–38

Finding Jesus in the Temple

Every year [Jesus'] parents used to go to Jerusalem for the feast of the Passover. When he was twelve years old, they went up for the feast as usual. When the days of the feast were over and they set off home, the boy Jesus stayed behind in Jerusalem without his parents knowing it. They assumed he was somewhere in the party, and it was only after a day's journey that they went to look for him among their relations and acquaintances. When they failed to find him they went back to Jerusalem looking for him everywhere.

It happened that, three days later, they found him in the Temple, sitting among the teachers, listening to them, and asking them questions; and all those who heard him were astounded at his intelligence and his replies. They were overcome when they saw him, and his mother said to him, "My child, why have you done this to us? See how worried your father and I have been, looking for you." He replied, "Why were you looking for me? Did you not know that I must be in my Father's house?" But they did not understand what he meant.

He went down with them and came to Nazareth and lived under their authority. His mother stored up all these things in her heart. And Jesus increased in wisdom, in stature, and in favor with God and with people.

—Luke 2:41–52

Jesus' Agony in the Garden

[Jesus and his disciples] came to a plot of land called Gethsemane, and he said to his disciples, "Stay here while I pray." Then he took Peter and James and John with him. And he began to feel terror and anguish. And he said to them, "My soul is sorrowful to the point of death. Wait here, and stay awake." And going on a little further he threw himself on the ground and prayed that, if it were possible, this hour might pass him by. "Abba, Father!" he said, "For you everything is possible. Take this cup away from me. But let it be as you, not I, would have it." He came back and found them sleeping, and he said to Peter, "Simon, are you asleep? Had you not the strength to stay awake one hour? Stay awake and pray not to be put to the test. The spirit is willing enough, but human nature is weak." Again he went away and prayed, saying the same words. And once more he came back and found them sleeping, their eyes were so heavy; and they could find no answer for him. He came back a third time and said to them, "You can sleep on now and have your rest. It is all over. The hour has come. Now the Son of man is to be betrayed into the hands of sinners. Get up! Let us go! My betrayer is not far away."

—Mark 14:32–42

Then Jesus came with [his disciples] to a plot of land called Gethsemane; and he said to his disciples, "Stay here while I go over there to pray." He took Peter and the two sons of Zebedee with him. And he began to feel sadness and anguish.

Then he said to them, "My soul is sorrowful to the point of death. Wait here and stay awake with me." And going on a little further he fell on his face and prayed. "My Father," he said, "if it is possible, let this cup pass me by. Nevertheless, let it be as you, not I, would have it." He came back to the disciples and found them sleeping, and he said to Peter, "So you had not the strength to stay awake with me for one hour? Stay awake, and pray not to be put to the test. The spirit is willing enough, but human nature is weak." Again, a second time, he went away and prayed: "My Father," he said, "if this cup cannot pass by, but I must drink it, your will be done!" And he came back again and found them sleeping, their eyes were so heavy. Leaving them there, he went away again and prayed for the third time, repeating the same words. Then he came back to the disciples and said to them, "You can sleep on now and have your rest. Look, the hour has come when the Son of man is to be betrayed into the hands of sinners. Get up! Let us go! Look, my betrayer is not far away."

—Matt. 26:36–46

Jesus then left [the upper room] to make his way as usual to the Mount of Olives, with the disciples following. When he reached the place he said to them, "Pray not to be put to the test."

Then he withdrew from them, about a stone's throw away, and knelt down and prayed. "Father," he said, "if you are willing, take this cup away from me. Nevertheless, let your will be done, not mine." Then an angel appeared to him, coming from heaven to give him strength. In his anguish he prayed even more earnestly, and his sweat fell to the ground like great drops of blood.

When he rose from prayer he went to the disciples and found them sleeping for sheer grief. And he said to them, "Why are you asleep? Get up and pray not to be put to the test."

—Luke 22:39–46

Jesus Is Scourged

So Pilate, anxious to placate the crowd, released Barabbas.for them and, after having Jesus scourged, he handed him over to be crucified.

—Mark 15:15

After having Jesus scourged he handed him over to be crucified.

—Matt. 27:26

Pilate then had Jesus taken away and scourged.

—John 19:1

Jesus Is Crowned with Thorns

The soldiers led him away to the inner part of the palace, that is, the Praetorium, and called the whole cohort together. They dressed him up in purple, twisted some thorns into a crown and put it on him. And they began saluting him, "Hail, king of the Jews!" They struck his head with a reed and spat on him; and they went down on their knees to do him homage. And when they had finished making fun of him, they took off the purple and dressed him in his own clothes.

—Mark 15:16–20

The governor's soldiers took Jesus with them into the Praetorium and collected the whole cohort round him. And they stripped him and put a scarlet cloak round him, and having twisted some thorns into a crown they put this on his head and placed a reed in his right hand. To make fun of him they knelt to him saying, "Hail, king of the Jews!" And they spat on him and took the reed and struck him on the head with it. And when they had finished making fun of him, they took off the cloak and dressed him in his own clothes and led him away to crucifixion.

—Matt. 27:27–31

The soldiers twisted some thorns into a crown and put it on his head and dressed him in a purple robe. They kept coming up to him and saying, "Hail, king of the Jews!" and slapping him in the face.

Pilate came outside again and said to them, "Look, I am going to bring him out to you to let you see that I find no case against him." Jesus then came out wearing the crown of thorns and the purple robe. Pilate said, "Here is the man." When they saw him, the chief priests and the guards shouted, "Crucify him! Crucify him!"

—John 19:2–6

Jesus Goes to Calvary

[The soldiers] led Jesus out to crucify him. They enlisted a passer-by, Simon of Cyrene, father of Alexander and Rufus, who was coming in from the country, to carry his cross. They brought Jesus to the place called Golgotha, which means the place of the skull.

—Mark 15:20–22

On their way out, the soldiers came across a man from Cyrene, called Simon and enlisted him to carry [Jesus'] cross.

—Matt. 27:32

As [the soldiers] were leading Jesus away they seized on a man, Simon from Cyrene, who was coming in from the country, and made him shoulder the cross and carry it behind Jesus. Large numbers of people followed him, and women too, who mourned and lamented for him. But Jesus turned to them and said, "Daughters of Jerusalem, do not weep for me; weep rather for yourselves and for your children. For look, the days are surely coming when people will say, 'Blessed are those who are barren, the wombs that have never borne children, the breasts that have never suckled!' Then they will begin to say to the mountains, 'Fall on us!'; to the hills, 'Cover us!' For if this is what is done to green wood, what will be done when the wood is dry?" Now they were also leading out two others, criminals, to be executed with him.

—Luke 23:26–32

[The Jews] then took charge of Jesus, and carrying his own cross he went out to the Place of the Skull or, as it is called in Hebrew, Golgotha.

—John 19:16–17

Jesus' Crucifixion

[The soldiers] offered [Jesus] wine mixed with myrrh, but he refused it. Then they crucified him, and shared out his clothing, casting lots to decide what each should get. It was the third hour when they crucified him. The inscription giving the charge against him read, "The King of the Jews." And they crucified two bandits with him, one on his right and one on his left.

The passers-by jeered at him; they shook their heads and said, "Aha! So you would destroy the Temple and rebuild it in three days! Then save yourself; come down from the cross!" The chief priests and the scribes mocked him among themselves in the same way with the words, "He saved others, he cannot save himself. Let the Christ, the king of Israel, come down from the cross now, for us to see it and believe." Even those who were crucified with him taunted him.

When the sixth hour came there was darkness over the whole land until the ninth hour. And at the ninth hour Jesus cried out in a loud voice, *"Eloi, eloi, lama sabachthani?"* which means, "My God, my God, why have you forsaken me?" When some of those who stood by heard this, they said, "Listen, he is calling on Elijah." Someone ran and soaked a sponge in vinegar and, putting it on a reed, gave it to him to drink saying, "Wait! And see if Elijah will come to take him down." But Jesus gave a loud cry and breathed his last. And the veil of the Sanctuary was torn in two from top to bottom. The centurion, who was standing in front of him, had seen how he had died, and he said, "In truth this man was the Son of God."

There were some women watching from a distance. Among them were Mary of Magdala, Mary who was the mother of James the younger and Joset, and Salome. These used to follow him and look after him when he was in Galilee. And many other women were there who had come up to Jerusalem with him.

—Mark 15:23–41

When [the soldiers] had reached a place called Golgotha, that is, the place of the skull, they gave him wine to drink mixed with gall, which he tasted but refused to drink. When they had finished crucifying him they shared out his clothing by casting lots, and then sat down and stayed there keeping guard over him.

Above his head was placed the charge against him; it read: "This is Jesus, the King of the Jews." Then two bandits were crucified with him, one on the right and one on the left.

The passers-by jeered at him; they shook their heads and said, "So you would destroy the Temple and in three days rebuild it! Then save yourself if you are God's son and come down from the cross!" The chief priests with the scribes and elders mocked him in the same way, with the words, "He saved others; he cannot save himself. He is the king of Israel; let him come down from the cross now, and we will believe in him. He has put his trust in God; now let God rescue him if he wants him. For he did say, 'I am God's son.' " Even the bandits who were crucified with him taunted him in the same way.

From the sixth hour there was darkness over all the land until the ninth hour. And about the ninth hour, Jesus cried out in a loud voice, "*Eli, eli, lama sabachthani?*" that is, "My God, my God, why have you forsaken me?" When some of those who stood there heard this, they said, "The man is calling on Elijah," and one of them ran quickly to get a sponge which he filled with vinegar and, putting it on a reed, gave it him to drink. But the rest of them said, "Wait! And see if Elijah will come to save him." But Jesus, again crying out in a loud voice, yielded up his spirit.

And suddenly, the veil of the Sanctuary was torn in two from top to bottom, the earth quaked, the rocks were split, the tombs opened and the bodies of many holy people rose from the dead, and these, after his resurrection, came out of tombs, entered the holy city and appeared to a number of people. The centurion, together with the others guarding Jesus, had seen the earthquake and all that was taking place, and they were terrified and said, "In truth this man was the son of God."

And many women were there, watching from a distance, the same women who had followed Jesus from Galilee and looked after him. Among them were Mary of Magdala, Mary the mother of James and Joseph, and the mother of Zebedee's sons.

—*Matt. 27:33–56*

When [the soldiers] reached the place called The Skull, there they crucified [Jesus] and the two criminals, one on his right, the other on his left. Jesus said, "Father, forgive them; they do not know what they are doing." Then they cast lots to share out his clothing.

The people stayed there watching. As for the leaders, they jeered at him with the words, "He saved others, let him save himself if he is the Christ of God, the Chosen One." The soldiers mocked him too, coming up to him, offering him vinegar, and saying, "If you are the king of the Jews, save yourself." Above him there was an inscription: "This is the King of the Jews."

One of the criminals hanging there abused him: "Are you not the Christ? Save yourself and us as well." But the other spoke up and rebuked him. "Have you no fear of God at all?" he said. "You got the same sentence as he did, but in our case we deserved it: we are paying for what we did. But this man has done nothing wrong." Then he said, "Jesus, remember me when you come into your kingdom." He answered him, "In truth I tell you, today you will be with me in paradise."

It was now about the sixth hour and the sun's light failed, so that darkness came over the whole land until the ninth hour. The veil of the Sanctuary was torn right down the middle. Jesus cried out in a loud voice saying, "Father, into your hands I commit my spirit." With these words he breathed his last.

When the centurion saw what had taken place, he gave praise to God and said, "Truly, this was an upright man." And when all the crowds who had gathered for the spectacle saw what had happened, they went home beating their breasts.

All his friends stood at a distance; so also did the women who had accompanied him from Galilee and saw all this happen.

—Luke 23:33–48

[The soldiers] crucified Jesus with two others, one on either side, Jesus being in the middle. Pilate wrote out a notice and had it fixed to the cross; it ran: "Jesus the Nazarene, King of the Jews." This notice was read by many of the Jews, because the place where Jesus was crucified was near the city and the writing was in Hebrew, Latin and Greek. So the Jewish chief priests said to Pilate, "You should not write 'King of the Jews,' but that the man said, 'I am King of the Jews.' " Pilate answered, "What I have written, I have written."

When the soldiers finished crucifying Jesus they took his clothing and divided it into four shares, one for each soldier. His undergarment was seamless, woven in one piece from neck to hem; so they said to one another, "Instead of tearing it, let's throw dice to decide who is to have it." In this way the words of scripture were fulfilled:

They divided my garments among them
and cast lots for my clothes.

That is what the soldiers did.

Near the cross of Jesus stood his mother and his mother's
sister, Mary the wife of Clopas, and Mary of Magdala. Seeing
his mother and the disciple whom he loved standing near her,
Jesus said to his mother, "Woman, this is your son." Then to the
disciple he said, "This is your mother." And from that hour the
disciple took her into his home.

After this, Jesus knew that everything had now been completed and, so that the scripture should be completely fulfilled,
he said:

I am thirsty.

A jar full of sour wine stood there; so, putting a sponge soaked
in the wine on a hyssop stick, they held it up to his mouth. After
Jesus had taken the wine he said, "It is fulfilled"; and bowing his
head he gave up his spirit.

—John 19:18–30

Jesus' Resurrection

When the Sabbath was over, Mary of Magdala, Mary the mother of James, and Salome brought spices with which to go and anoint him. And very early in the morning on the first day of the week they went to the tomb when the sun had risen.

They had been saying to one another, "Who will roll away the stone for us from the entrance of the tomb?" But when they looked they saw that the stone—which was very big—had already been rolled back. On entering the tomb they saw a young man in a white robe seated on the right-hand side, and they were struck with amazement. But he said to them, "There is no need to be so amazed. You are looking for Jesus of Nazareth, who was crucified; he has risen, he is not here. See, here is the place where they had laid him. But you must go and tell his disciples and Peter, 'He is going ahead of you to Galilee; that is where you will see him, just as he told you.' " And the women came out and ran away from the tomb because they were frightened out of their wits; and they said nothing to anyone, for they were afraid.

Having risen in the morning on the first day of the week, he appeared first to Mary of Magdala from whom he had cast out seven devils. She then went to those who had been his companions, and who were mourning and in tears, and told them. But they did not believe her when they heard her say that he was alive and that she had seen him.

—Mark 16:1–11

After the Sabbath, and towards dawn on the first day of the week, Mary of Magdala and the other Mary went to visit the sepulcher. And suddenly there was a violent earthquake, for an angel of the Lord, descending from heaven, came and rolled away the stone and sat on it. His face was like lightning, his robe white as snow. The guards were so shaken by fear of him that they were like dead men. But the angel spoke; and he said to the women, "There is no need for you to be afraid. I know you are looking for Jesus, who was crucified. He is not here, for he has risen, as he said he would. Come and see the place where he lay, then go quickly and tell his disciples, 'He has risen from the dead and now he is going ahead of you to Galilee; that is where you will see him.' Look! I have told you." Filled with awe and great joy the women came quickly away from the tomb and ran to tell his disciples.

And suddenly, coming to meet them, was Jesus. "Greetings," he said. And the women came up to him and, clasping his feet, they did him homage. Then Jesus said to them, "Do not be afraid; go and tell my brothers that they must leave for Galilee; there they will see me."

—Matt. 28:1–10

On the first day of the week, at the first sign of dawn, [the women who followed Jesus] went to the tomb with the spices they had prepared. They found that the stone had been rolled away from the tomb, but on entering they could not find the body of the Lord Jesus. As they stood there puzzled about this, two men in brilliant clothes suddenly appeared at their side. Terrified, the women bowed their heads to the ground. But the two said to them, "Why look among the dead for someone who is alive? He is not here; he has risen. Remember what he told you when he was still in Galilee: that the Son of man was destined to be handed over into the power of sinful men and be crucified, and rise again on the third day." And they remembered his words.

And they returned from the tomb and told all this to the Eleven and to all the others. The women were Mary of Magdala, Joanna, and Mary the mother of James. And the other women with them also told the apostles, but this story of theirs seemed pure nonsense and they did not believe them.

Peter, however, went off to the tomb, running. He bent down and looked in and saw the linen cloths but nothing else; he then went back home, amazed at what had happened.

—Luke 24:1–12

They were still talking about all this when Jesus himself stood among them and said to them, "Peace be with you!" In a state of alarm and fright, they thought they were seeing a ghost. But he said, "Why are you so agitated, and why are these doubts stirring in your hearts? See by my hands and my feet that it is I myself. Touch me and see for yourselves; a ghost has no flesh and bones as you can see I have." And as he said this he showed them his hands and his feet. Their joy was so great that they still could not believe it, as they were dumbfounded; so he said to them, "Have you anything here to eat?" And they offered him a piece of grilled fish, which he took and ate before their eyes.

Then he told them, "This is what I meant when I said, while I was still with you, that everything written about me in the Law of Moses, in the Prophets and in the Psalms, was destined to be fulfilled." He then opened their minds to understand the scriptures, and he said to them, "So it is written that the Christ would suffer and on the third day rise from the dead, and that, in his name, repentance for the forgiveness of sins would be preached to all nations, beginning from Jerusalem. You are witnesses to this."

—Luke 24:36–48

It was very early on the first day of the week and still dark when Mary of Magdala came to the tomb. She saw that the stone had been moved away from the tomb and came running to Simon Peter and the other disciple, the one whom Jesus loved. "They have taken the Lord out of the tomb," she said, "and we don't know where they have put him."

So Peter set out with the other disciple to go to the tomb. They ran together, but the other disciple, running faster than Peter, reached the tomb first; he bent down and saw the linen cloths lying on the ground, but did not go in. Simon Peter, following him, also came up, went into the tomb, saw the linen cloths lying on the ground and also the cloth that had been over his head; this was not with the linen cloths but rolled up in a place by itself. Then the other disciple who had reached the tomb first also went in; he saw and he believed. Till this moment they had still not understood the scripture, that he must rise from the dead. The disciples then went back home.

But Mary was standing outside near the tomb, weeping. Then, as she wept, she stooped to look inside and saw two angels in white sitting where the body of Jesus had been, one at the head, the other at the feet. They said, "Woman, why are you weeping?" "They have taken my Lord away," she replied, "and I don't know where they have put him." As she said this she turned round and saw Jesus standing there, though she did not realize that it was Jesus. Jesus said to her, "Woman, why are you weeping? Who are you looking for?" Supposing him to be the gardener, she said, "Sir, if you have taken him away, tell me where you have put him and I will go and remove him." Jesus said, "Mary!" She turned round then and said to him in Hebrew, "*Rabbuni!*"—which means Master. Jesus said to her, "Do not cling to me, because I have not yet ascended to the Father.

But go to the brothers and tell them: I am ascending to my Father and your Father, to my God and your God." So Mary of Magdala told the disciples, "I have seen the Lord," and that he had said these things to her.

—John 20:1–18

Jesus' Ascension into Heaven

And so the Lord Jesus, after he had spoken to [the apostles], was taken up into heaven; there at the right hand of God he took his place, while they, going out, preached everywhere, the Lord working with them and confirming the word by the signs that accompanied it.

—Mark 16:19–20

Then [Jesus] took [the apostles] out as far as the outskirts of Bethany and, raising his hands, he blessed them. Now as he blessed them, he withdrew from them and was carried up to heaven. They worshiped him and then went back to Jerusalem full of joy; and they were continually in the Temple praising God.

—Luke 24:50–53

Now having met together, the apostles asked Jesus, "Lord, has the time come for you to restore the kingdom to Israel?" He replied, "It is not for you to know times or dates that the Father has decided by his own authority, but you will receive the power of the Holy Spirit which will come on you, and then you will be my witnesses not only in Jerusalem but throughout Judaea and Samaria, and indeed to earth's remotest end."

As he said this he was lifted up while they looked on, and a cloud took him from their sight. They were still staring into the sky as he went, when suddenly two men in white were standing beside them, and they said, "Why are you Galileans standing here looking into the sky? This Jesus who has been taken up from you into heaven will come back in the same way as you have seen him go into heaven."

So from the Mount of Olives, as it is called, they went back to Jerusalem, a short distance away, no more than a Sabbath walk.

—Acts 1:6–12

The Descent of the Holy Spirit
on the Apostles

When Pentecost day came round, [the disciples] had all met together, when suddenly there came from heaven a sound as of a violent wind which filled the entire house in which they were sitting; and there appeared to them tongues as of fire; these separated and came to rest on the head of each of them. They were all filled with the Holy Spirit and began to speak different languages as the Spirit gave them power to express themselves.

Now there were devout men living in Jerusalem from every nation under heaven, and at this sound they all assembled, and each one was bewildered to hear these men speaking his own language. They were amazed and astonished. "Surely," they said, "all these men speaking are Galileans? How does it happen that each of us hears them in his own native language? Parthians, Medes and Elamites; people from Mesopotamia, Judaea and Cappadocia, Pontus and Asia, Phrygia and Pamphylia, Egypt and the parts of Libya round Cyrene; residents of Rome—Jews and proselytes alike—Cretans and Arabs, we hear them preaching in our own language about the marvels of God." Everyone was amazed and perplexed; they asked one another what it all meant. Some, however, laughed it off. "They have been drinking too much new wine," they said.

Then Peter stood up with the Eleven and addressed them in a loud voice: "Men of Judaea, and all you who live in Jerusalem, make no mistake about this, but listen carefully to what I say. These men are not drunk, as you imagine; why, it is only the third hour of the day. On the contrary, this is what the prophet was saying:

In the last days—the Lord declares—I shall pour out my Spirit on all humanity. Your sons and daughters shall prophesy, your young people shall see visions, your old people dream dreams. Even on the slaves, men and women, shall I pour out my Spirit. I will show portents in the sky above and signs on the earth below. The sun will be turned into darkness and the moon into blood before the day of the Lord comes, that great and terrible Day. And all who call on the name of the Lord will be saved.

—Acts 2:1-21

The Assumption and Coronation
of the Blessed Virgin Mary

Now a great sign appeared in heaven: a woman, robed with the
sun, standing on the moon, and on her head a crown of twelve
stars. . . . The woman was delivered of a boy, the son who was
to rule all the nations with an iron scepter, and the child was
taken straight up to God and to his throne. . . .

As soon as the dragon found himself hurled down to the
earth, he sprang in pursuit of the woman, the mother of the
male child, but she was given a pair of the great eagle's wings
to fly away from the serpent. . . . Then the dragon was enraged
with the woman and went away to make war on the rest of her
children, who obey God's commandments and have in themselves the witness of Jesus.

—Rev. 12:1–17

6

The Fifteen Mysteries

Even though it belongs to all of us, the rosary is an intensely private prayer. It opens the way for us to enter personally into each of its mysteries. Each time we take the beads in hand, we are invited anew to experience these most significant moments, to be present as they unfold—unfold historically, but also mystically in our lives today.

As I was writing this book for you, I received an unexpected grace: I was able to spend some days in the Holy Land. As I went about, I visited the actual site where each of the mysteries took place. At each site I sought to let the appropriate mystery be present to me, and then I wrote some thoughts on it. It is these thoughts that I now share with you. They are seminal thoughts only; so much more could be written on each of the mysteries, so many more aspects explored. May these thoughts open the way for you to do that during your daily rosary.

The Annunciation
Nazareth

The Basilica of the Annunciation is a good place to begin. A church built on many levels, it contains homes from the time of Jesus, an early Christian place of worship, a Constantinian basilica, the enormous basilica of the Crusaders, and today's strikingly modern edifice, which rises above all its surroundings. The event that traditionally took place here has drawn forth the talents of every succeeding age. Men and women of great talent have expressed their meditations on this mystery in stone, mosaic, and paint, uncovering the many levels of the mystery itself. As I sit here writing, groups of pilgrims pass by speaking the languages of many nations. This mystery belongs to all people of all times, each assimilating and living it in his or her own way according to each one's particular grace.

I sit opposite the little grotto that traditionally covers the site of the home of Joachim and Anna. Beneath the altar, pilgrims bend to kiss the marble stone: *Hic Verbum caro factum est.* "Here the Word was made flesh."

I am a bit weary from the long, hot journey. Things did not all go as I would have liked, so I have some remaining feelings of anger, self-pity, and hurt. How out of place these all seem in the face of this awesome mystery: God coming to us in our very own humanity. But this is what it is all about. He became one of us, like us in all but sin yet taking on even our sin so that he could heal all of this. If I am to give him my humanity, it has to be this poor, needy, weak, and sinful humanity. There is no other "me" to offer him now. It is crazy to think that we have to get all spruced up to offer ourselves to God. In fact, the only way we *can* get spruced up is by offering our mess to him.

One of the wonders of what took place here—and in sacramental mystery continues to take place here—is that one of us had a humanity to give him that was *not* messed up. But that was so only because, in a way that it took us a long time to understand, he "spruced up" Mary's humanity at the very instant it became hers.

I wonder, though, if Mary was not more conscious of unworthiness than we unworthy sinners are. Did not this little woman—barely more than a girl—who had faithfully pondered the Scriptures through the years and entered into the liturgies and rituals of her people (as much as a woman was allowed to) come to a deep sense of the awesomeness of Yahweh? Surely God had prepared Mary in a special way for this moment. Without some divine illumination she could never have grasped the angelic message sufficiently to give human assent. Yet any illumination concerning the Trinity—the fact that Yahweh is three in one, a Father who has a Son who by the action of their Holy Spirit will become in a completely human, physical way *her* son—must have made Yahweh even more awesome. "Mary, do not be afraid." Yet how fearsome is this mystery!

And how loving! For love is the whole motive and message. I do not know how Gabriel appeared to Mary, nor do I know if there is any way that an angel can suddenly be present to one of us without causing fright, at least until some reassuring words produce their effect. But the message that Gabriel brought, with its concomitant illumination, could *never* be less than awesome and fearsome. It is a mystery that prostrates even the highest angels in awe: God in his compassionate love truly becomes human!

Here is yet more wonder: God wants, in his compassionate love, to become human so that he can heal us humans with gentleness and humble care. (This thought staggers me as I write it.) And yet God does not impose on us his wants—even though they are totally to our good. Rather, he humbly asks our assent. And the best of us, the only sinless one among us, is here to speak for us all and welcome him.

Bernard of Clairvaux dramatically depicts the annunciation in one of his sermons. Angels and ancestors stand on tiptoes, as it were, in anxious expectation. All who went before and all who will come after, all humanity and all heaven, await Mary's yes. And how beautifully she expresses it: "You see before you the Lord's servant, let it happen to me as you have said." If only I can live that. If only that can become my heartfelt and whole-hearted response to all that God asks and allows in my life.

Yet Mary did not *immediately* say that. First she had a question. The Lord is not put off by our questions and struggles, if underneath them lies a disposition to say yes when by his grace things become sufficiently clear.

"Let it happen to me as you have said"—for that I pray in this mystery.

Let me fully accept my humanity. Let me be ever more filled with awe at his divinity and at that divine love that has so embraced my humanity.

Our Father . . .

The Visitation
En Karem

En Karem. Even today, in an air-conditioned car, the journey from Nazareth to En Karem (southeast of Jerusalem) is not an easy one: heat, dust, the bleakness of desert and desolate land, and the pervasive sense of hostility in Samaria. All that has not changed much. And even when one reaches the village, the journey is not over. The church on the outskirts that stands on the site of the home of Elizabeth and Zechariah is difficult to find, nestled high on one of the ascents toward Jerusalem.

But now I sit in the beautiful courtyard. Flowers of all sorts dance in the sunny breeze. Opposite me are the remains of the medieval church, with a modern tower that reaches high over the new sandstone church. Behind me on the wall are ceramic plaques with Mary's *Magnificat* in forty-four languages.

Mary's coming here was her first concrete expression of the faith she placed in God and in his angel's message. And it is that faith that is magnified here. "Blessed is she who believed." Later Jesus, when a woman proclaimed his mother happy in hearing him, praised even more her faith.

Like Mary's, our faith needs to be expressed first and concretely in our outreach to others. Our faith needs to be constantly nurtured with prayer and Scripture, as Mary's was, but faith without works is dead. "How can we say we love God whom we cannot see, when we don't love our sisters and brothers whom we do see?" "Whatever you do for the least of mine you do for me." Jesus comes to us in the poor and needy, in our relatives and family, in every human person. We live our faith by responding to each person as Christ—with reverence, love, and care.

Mary lived great faith, making the long journey from Nazareth. As she trudged down the rough roads, I am sure that she did not dwell on the heat and fatigue, the lack of privacy, even the constant danger—though she must have been well aware of all these things. She was intent on her cousin, with her need, and on the divine within her. She brought not just human love, concern, and care to those to whom she came; she brought divine life and love. So do we, for God lives and loves within us. This is the important thing. We should not be so concerned about the material help we bring others that we let it obscure everything else and leave no room for divine love to shine through.

The divine love did indeed shine forth when Mary came. The sound of her voice called forth prophecy; a child even in the darkness of the womb leaped for joy. Thus did Mary's specialness shine forth and receive prophetic acclaim. And what was Mary's response to this? So often when someone praises the beautiful work of God in us, we seek to deny it or make little of it in a distorted kind of humility. Not so Mary. "My soul proclaims the greatness of the Lord. . . . All generations will call me blessed." She is the greatest, and she knows it. She knows the Source of that greatness, and she honors it: "The almighty has done great things for me. Holy is his name."

En Karem, the visitation, is faith—concrete faith expressed in care and love for each other. It is true humility—the humility of truth. We are great, and we sometimes act according to our greatness. And it is all by his grace, because the almighty does great things for us. Holy is his name.

Our Father . . .

The Birth of Jesus
Bethlehem

The cave is still warm. Today one group of pilgrims after another crowds into it. They light their candles, kiss the star under the altar, listen to the gospel, and sing hymns in many languages. It is sad both that Jesus had to turn to the warm earth and humble animals for welcome, because no human heart was warm enough to provide room for him, and that humans today pay their curious tribute even while they desecrate his earth and abuse his animals for their own selfish ends.

At least we are all impelled to bend our proud necks to come here. The large door of the basilica was blocked many centuries ago (so that Muslims could not ride their horses inside), and each pilgrim must now bow low and edge his or her way in. Fitting indeed. The wonder of it! Our God—*God himself*—bowed down. He—God—was born in a cave. The displaced, the dispossessed, who live in great numbers in similar surroundings all over the world today, can find some comfort in knowing that God so loves them that he became one of them. An alien government that worshiped its own fabricated gods dominated the Newborn's mother and her husband and dragged them from their home and daily work, from their peaceful life at such a crucial moment in it. But sad to say, even worse tyranny on the part of their own puppet ruler would send them fleeing for their lives into an alien land. Is there anything we suffer that Jesus did not also suffer?

Most of us suffer another kind of exile—an exile from ourselves, from our own true selves. We live in self-alienation. Can coming to the manger heal this? There is nothing in the human experience that Jesus did not accept and even embrace. Can we not learn from him to accept and embrace all the reality of our own lives instead of creating a false self and hiding within it even from ourselves? If God himself can embrace all that is human and still be all holy, all good, and all beautiful, why should we fear any of the human elements of our lives? In embracing humanity in his own life, Jesus embraced it in our lives as well, with an embrace of transforming love. All is healed. All is transformed. All is capable of divinity. All that we have to do is accept all that is human within us as our own and bring it to him. The shepherds brought sheep and the smells of the sheepfold as well as the aura of the outcast. The Magi brought gold and the rich perfumes of the East as well as the awesomeness of the powerful. Jesus accepted it all. He will accept all that we bring.

The pilgrims continue to come. Only God knows what each one brings, and with what kind of heart. We come mystically to the cave. We know the mess that we bring and the often distracted heart that brings it. This is all we have—all we *are*. Let us now bring it to the Lord. And the loving Little One stretches out his arms to receive us. A smiling mother encourages. A watchful Joseph guides.

With confidence we pray.

Our Father . . .

The Presentation of Jesus in the Temple
Jerusalem: The Temple Mount

The journey from Bethlehem to Jerusalem is not a long one—six or seven miles—though long enough a walk for a young mother who had given birth only forty days earlier and for a young father carrying that most precious of sons. The golden walls of Jerusalem appear soon enough, then the walls of the Temple and the great Golden Gate, closed now almost since the days when the Son of man last passed through them.

The Temple is quiet today. There are few pilgrims. Strikes and fear of war keep them away. Because no one knows exactly how the vast Temple area was laid out before the destruction, Jews now are not supposed to enter the area, lest they step within what was the Holy of Holies. Mary and Joseph would have brought the Child through the Court of the Gentiles and the Court of the Women to the entrance of the Court of the Israelites, where Simeon would have met them. That holy old man took the Child into his arms: "Now you can dismiss your servant, O Lord. . . ."

How powerfully the Holy Spirit has worked in this just man! All he wanted was the fulfillment of the promises of his God. May the Lord work such purity of heart in me that I can, without hesitation, recognize the Holy One of God in each man, woman, and child. And may I long only for the fulfillment of the promises of God among all his people in my lifetime.

The solid golden stones, radiant in the noonday sun, speak of solidity, assurance, and unshakable faith in the Presence and the Promise. How sad that today they are sacred to three religions that divide the one redeemed people of God into warring camps. Simeon's dreadful prophecy is fulfilled beyond all expectation: "He is destined for the fall and the rise of many in Israel, destined to be a sign that is opposed."

"A sword will pierce your soul too." The very words were the first piercing. And within days there would be flight in the night, exile, the life of a displaced family seeking sanctuary. In years to come the unfolding mission of her Son would send the shaft deeper and deeper. She would come to these precincts, searching, with all the fears of a mother. Later she would hear the talk, the rumors, see the aftermath of his words and actions. And finally she would have her part in the horror that would begin to unfold in the Antonianum at the corner of this great Temple.

The Temple was the glory of the people. The psalms sing of it again and again. How bittersweet became Mary's joy in it. The fulfillment of all that the Temple stood for among God's people came that day when she and Joseph carried in the King of Glory, hidden in the form of a Little One, a poor Little One who was worth the ransom of a young pigeon. Faith saw and prophetically joined the lament. For the rest, his coming made no apparent difference.

The whole world is God's Temple. He has come and dwells in it. For most, it seems to make little or no difference. Does it make as much difference in my life as it should? Do I hear Simeon's words, and Anna's? Are Mary's sorrows a reality for me?

I come into the Temple today with Mary and Joseph and Jesus. I am a pleasing offering to the Father, because I am offered by them, one with Jesus. Anna and Simeon are still here, the just ones among us—still praying and interceding for the people, for us all. We pray with them now.

Our Father . . .

Finding Jesus in the Temple
Jerusalem: At the Western Wall of the Temple

Things change yet ever remain the same. In the caverns along the west wall of the Temple, hundreds of men and boys of all ages are gathered. Some are intent upon their prayer, standing close to the wall or sitting, bowing, and shifting. Others gather in groups, chanting as they sway rhythmically. Some sit in twos or threes, earnestly discussing the Scriptures; at times they even seem to be arguing. How easy it would have been for young Jesus to stay behind for days in a crowd like this. There are many here twelve years of age or younger. Just a few feet from me two young people arrive with their schoolbags, find two chairs and draw them together, take out their books, and become immediately engrossed in discussion. They can be only twelve or thirteen, if that. Another youngster wanders by obviously in search of someone—perhaps his father or a rebbe. The cadences of sound rise and fall.

And Jewish mothers are Jewish mothers. They may not be allowed to enter this precinct of men, but they hover outside in their own area. These are a communal people. The rabbi has his flock. The extended family cares and can be trusted. No one seems to worry about the children who run about; they are in the care of all. No wonder Jesus' staying behind was not noticed until the evening of the first day's journey back.

But why did Jesus stay behind? "Did you not know that I must be in my Father's house?" What is he implying that Mary should have been aware of? He is a man now, by Jewish law. He has his rights and his duties and his responsibilities, yet he is still subject. He acknowledges this and lives it. Sometimes it is not so clear what we owe to God and what we owe to others: parents, superiors, hierarchs, civil authorities, our fellow humans. It was clear to Jesus, and he knew how to coordinate his responsibilities. Others did not understand—even his sinless mother. Later some were threatened by his clarity and even plotted his death. His mother, even in her pain—and free enough to give expression to some annoyance with God—only questioned.

We do not have to have all the answers. We may even feel annoyed with God and with the way he acts in our regard. Yet we need, in the end, to place our questions and plaints humbly before him.

Sometimes, though, we feel that he has walked out on us, abandoned us. He is not here to receive our plaints or hear our questions. What then? Like Mary, we seek him sorrowing. Maybe this is the more common experience in our lives: seeking an apparently absent God, wondering why he is treating us this way. We say our beads longing for his presence, for some answer to our questions.

Our Father . . .

Jesus' Agony in the Garden
Jerusalem: Gethsemane

We walk through the grove of ancient olive trees—offspring of those Jesus knew—into the large, dark, quiet basilica. Before the altar stretches an expanse of raw rock. Is this the rock washed by the sweaty blood of our Savior? Certainly this is the garden where he came for the greatest struggle of his life.

Jesus is completely human even while he is completely divine. He is the most highly sensitive of humans in his humanity and in his faith. Prophetic foresight only augmented his suffering. In the coming few hours he would undergo physical abuse beyond anything I can get hold of. It is enough to make him sweat blood. But on top of the physical anguish there is so much more. He is a man; he wants and needs his friends. He needs human support. How densely insensitive we are. We avoid being with him in his passion and prayer in the agonies of our sisters and brothers today—if not by sleep then by unawareness, other occupations, and cultivated distractions. We do not have time to watch with him for an hour, but we have time for hours of television or chatting with friends. "Could you not watch one hour with me?" The friars at this Basilica of All Nations invite each of us to watch in union with them for one hour the first Thursday of each month as they watch here in Gethsemane with Jesus.

Horrible physical abuse, degradation, abandonment, and piercing loneliness are not the whole sum of it for Jesus; in fact, they are the least part. For this Son, who so loves to be before the Father, who so loves the Father, now stands before him with all our sin. He will be left to experience abandonment and separation even from the Father. I, who have such a meager sense of what sin is, can in no wise conceive of this agony.

Lord, as I kneel here and see you, the great Strong One, cry out, "Father, if it be possible, let this chalice pass me by," help me to begin to perceive what is sin, what is my sin before your Father—the Father so good, so merciful, so loving, who is also my father. Lord, it is time to pray, to let your Spirit form in me a new mind and heart—one more sensitive to the fullness of reality, to sin, to redeeming love, to grace, to who you are, to who I am in you. Give me the grace and the courage to watch, if not one hour right now, at least one decade, to let the reality form my mind and heart.

Our Father . . .

Jesus Is Scourged
Jerusalem: The Chapel of the Flagellation

It is all covered now by churches and schools and other institutions. Save for some stones in the floors of the churches and in the excavations, little can be seen from Jesus' time and experience. But here, perhaps many feet or yards down, the most precious blood flowed out, stained the paving stones, seeped into some crevices, and consecrated this soil forever. Bits of sacred flesh, as sacred as that which I ate at the altar this morning, spattered about, torn out by whips of leather and bone.

That flesh and blood is honored in these buildings, hidden under sacramental veils in tabernacles of gold. The hiddenness of Christ. Hidden in pain and humiliation. A Palestinian, seeking to keep his dignity by offering some little service for some little payment, was hovering at the gate as I entered. I impolitely ignored him. He trailed after me, giving his little speech. I knelt in prayer in the Chapel of the Flagellation, hoping that he would go away. But he hung on. There are very few pilgrims these days, with the threat of war hanging over the city. As I prayed, I looked down and saw in the marble a haggard face. *Your* face, telling me again that you are one with your poor and suffering. I rose from my prayer and took some pictures. Still my unwanted guide hung on. I explained that I wanted to write and sat down to do so, but he hovered nearby, willing to wait. Finally, I fished out a dollar and sent him off. He said that he would wait at the gate to show me more. As he went away, it hit me: this man is Christ!

Lord, when will I begin to see? I am ashamed now. Lord, open my eyes. There is always time and space for reverence, respect, kindness. Lord, forgive me. Lord, do I not scourge you when I treat you as I just treated my Palestinian brother? Forgive me. Help me to learn.

I cannot meditate long on your physical scourging. It is too unreal for me—too horrible. Horrible, too, the dehumanization of the men who so scourged you. I know that you forgave them, for they did not know what they were doing, these homesick, bored young brutes, given too much power before they could handle it responsibly. It happens again and again in our militarized nations. And I know that you forgive me when I do not realize what I am doing. We need to let the horror of your scourging sink more deeply into our flesh, into our consciousness, so that we will become more and more mindful, caring, aware. Lord, help us. May your every wound be cut into our souls and hearts, until we live compassion, *are* compassion. Lord, help.

Our Father . . .

Jesus Is Crowned with Thorns
Jerusalem: The Praetorium

They call it Losthrotrotos—the Place of the Pavement. Here in the courtyard of the Fortress of the Antonianum the sadistic young Roman soldiers took Jesus in hand. He had been condemned to death. His life was worth nothing; he was theirs for sport. The heavy stones of the pavement still show the forms of the different games they played here to wile away the time. Little did those "playful" young men know that the one they played with that day was the very Son of God. Little do the young soldiers of today know that the men, women, and children they so brutalize are in fact the children of God—one with the very Son of God.

As we enter the excavations, the Sisters of Sion who care for them have two slide projectors casting images on the wall, side by side. One projects a collection of classical representations of Christ in paint, glass, mosaic, and sculpture. The other projects Christ today in all his sufferings: prison, war, hospital ward, hunger, homelessness, abuse of every kind.

Jesus suffered much here in the Praetorium. He who in humility knew his own dignity knew the enormity of the irreverence in this mock reverence. Yet still more his heart bled for these magnificent young men whom he had made, who were so locked into their bored desperation that they had no sense of their own magnificence. He knew how transformed their lives could be if they but knew who it was they mocked, if that mock reverence were turned into true reverence. But he had to allow this to be for now. It all somehow had its place in the mysterious plan of the Father.

Jesus suffered much here. He suffers much today, in so many places, in so many ways. He who could summon twelve legions of angels, who could simply let all this faulted creation cease to share in his being, quietly let his creatures mock him then—still lets them mock today.

They strip him, tearing his flayed flesh yet more. He is totally exposed. Then a rough cloak is thrown over him, further abusing his shredded body. The slaps! The jeers! The spittle! Finally the thorns—and the blows that drive them more deeply into his head.

God, has there ever been such suffering?

And yet it is *meekly* borne. How that goes against my male arrogance. I have a lot to learn from you, Meek and Humble of Heart. Teach me. And give me the courage to live what you teach.

Our Father . . .

Jesus Goes to Calvary
Jerusalem: The *Via Dolorosa*

The artistic and rather antiseptic tableaux in our churches prepare us not at all for the experience of making the stations of the cross in Jerusalem. Here they are totally immersed in life. The judgment takes place in what is now a Muslim schoolyard. The journey wends down narrow, shop-lined streets along the north and then the west side of the Temple area before striking off up Golgotha. Some stations are marked by little chapels set in the respective buildings; others are but a mark on the wall. As we make our way along, life goes on as usual. Shops are busy; merchants try to sell us all sorts of religious trinkets and many other things. Children rush about us in their games. Older Muslims and Jews belligerently push their way through our praying throng. Some make rude noises, but most simply ignore us.

And so it was when Jesus first made this journey. Curiosity caused some to stop and look as the criminals were led out. But most took little notice while the Son of God went forth to die for them. A few friends and a crowd of dedicated enemies followed. A stranger was forced to help, carrying the heavy cross — too heavy now for a man who has been so brutalized (even if he *is* God).

I want to be Simon and help my cruelly battered Lord. I am tempted to envy Veronica her sacred image — but Jesus imprints that image in each one of us. Above all I would have Mary's compassion.

What more can be said? It is all too brutal, too incomprehensible. This is *God* who stumbles and falls and lies prostrate under a piece of wood. As a carpenter, he was well practiced in carrying beams. But then he was a strapping young man. Now

he is a beaten man—hungry, tired, cold and hot, his body
abused beyond anything my imagination can picture (and I
worked with lepers in India and starving families in Haiti).
"Have you seen any sorrow like my sorrow?"
No, Lord. And I know that each bloody step that is so deliberately and painfully placed on that ascent to Calvary is in
reparation for all the times I have *not* walked in the ways of the
Father. Lord, forgive me. It is wondrous that in your most
awful pain you can yet think of others; you can stop and console
those who would console you. What promise this gives of your
compassion for me, who wants to help you as Simon did and
yet is so often enticed from the way—and thereby only increases
your burden.

Such Love! Such love! Even in giving all for me, you ex-
panded your sufferings to give me totally undeserved signs of
your understanding (you fell three times; you understand falls),
signs of your compassion. Thank you so much, so very much.
Give us the grace to walk more fully with you.

Our Father . . .

Jesus' Crucifixion
Jerusalem: Church of the Holy Sepulcher,
Mount Calvary

Calvary! The narrow steps are steep. It is a dark corner in the vast Basilica of Saint Savior, the Church of the Holy Sepulcher. Like everything else in Christendom, it is divided: half Roman Catholic, half Greek Orthodox.

Chants from a multitude of liturgies in a multitude of languages drift up from all parts of the basilica to form a sonorous cacophony. Hundreds of lamps bring the frescoes, mosaics, and gold-covered icons to life. On a bench near the railing a man sleeps peacefully, stretched out under a blanket. No one disturbs him. An Orthodox nun with an entourage from the women's auxiliary busily renews the lamps. A sleepy young Franciscan yawns and scratches as he awaits the end of a mass that an elderly Spaniard is celebrating with great fervor. Old women wearing black dresses and kerchiefs repeatedly prostrate themselves and then crawl under the altar to reach down and touch the actual stone of Calvary.

Should Calvary be like this? Perhaps so. After all, the passion of Christ was and is totally enmeshed in life, although our pictures and images too often set it apart. Christ's passion is the very center, the culmination, the summit of all creation, because it is the summit of human and divine love. Yet it is within *all* aspects of creation—even the lowliest. It is the leaven that raises up, that makes all capable of being loved and worthy of the Father.

I stand here with John, the disciple whom Jesus loved, feeling helpless. There is a time for doing. And a time for being. And a time for being with. The three hours must have seemed an endless eternity—three hours standing at this spot, watching Jesus hang here, life flowing out, each breath more labored. There is nothing to do but let Jesus suffer and give all for us. This is difficult. We want so to affirm our worth and validity by *doing*. But we need to realize that ultimately it all comes from Jesus. Ours is to receive. There is much for us to do; but all that we are to do, can do, do do is by his grace and power, by what happens here on Calvary.

"Greater love than this . . ." Each moment that we stand here, watching Jesus, feeling with Jesus—at least in what little way we can—makes that love more of a reality in our lives. Lord, give us the grace and courage to stand more faithfully on Calvary.

Our Father . . .

Jesus' Resurrection
Jerusalem: Church of the Holy Sepulcher, the Empty Tomb

The great bell booms with such intensity that the whole basilica seems to vibrate. The different hierarchs are arriving for the great feast, each with his own procession of clerics and faithful. The liturgies will go on all morning, sending up their collective (and, sad to say, competitive) chants to the Throne of Mercy.

What strikes me most strongly in this great, multilayered church is that the center is not Calvary but this empty tomb — this empty tomb that is the very center of Christian faith. "If Christ has not been raised, your faith is pointless."

But he *has* been raised. The tomb is empty. One after another, priests and nuns, women and men, people of all ages, bend low and enter the dimly lighted chamber. They kneel and kiss the stone. Little attention is paid to the icons and frescoes. No, it is the emptiness that matters. He is not here. He is risen.

All the chambers of my heart, of my being, need to be emptied — even of beautiful images, the holy images — if the Reality is going to enter in and wholly possess me. But I cannot empty myself by my own efforts, because those very efforts fill me. I need to let the risen Lord come in with all his radiance, his enlightenment, which will disperse all my dark shadows and homemade images and totally fill me with the Reality. Paradoxically, it is by sitting in the darkness, letting go of my own little "lights," longing for the true light that enlightens all who come into the true light, that I come into the light, become myself light by his light.

Christ is risen. No matter what be the burden and darkness, the pain of my life, it is but for a time. Then resurrection, unending light, peace, and joy forever. Because he is risen. If I am open, if I am attentive, he will come in quiet moments, moments when I am fearful and alone, when I am about my work or enjoying a meal with friends. He will come again and again until I know that I, too, am risen—baptized into the risen Christ, one with him, already belonging to the heavenly places.

Lord, fill us with the grace and light of your risen life.

Now it is time to go into the tomb and experience the emptiness so that he can fill it.

Our Father . . .

Jesus' Ascension into Heaven
Jerusalem: The Church of the Ascension, Mount of Olives

Again, emptiness. The climb up Olivet is long and hot. We pass through the olive groves, then pass the Church of All Nations and the many-domed Russian Church of Saint Mary Magdalene. The teardrop chapel that marks the spot where Jesus wept over his city is set in a green oasis amid thousands of graves. Finally at the summit, we enter a low door and come to the plain stone dome that stands over the spot from which Jesus traditionally is said to have ascended. The little chapel is totally bare. Here, as elsewhere, the Muslims took over a site sacred to Jesus' memory, stripped it of all icons and frescoes, of all the rich Byzantine art, and then used it as a mosque. The minaret they built still stands by the entrance to the courtyard, a great circle within which stands the little circular and totally empty church. Emptiness.

There is a certain squalor about the place. A young Palestinian collects a shekel from everyone who enters. An Armenian patriarch celebrates here on certain feasts, but for the most part the church seems to be in the hands of a few young Palestinians, who try to sell some souvenirs and collect a little by way of admission.

I have the feeling, sitting here, that Jesus took off for heaven and forsook his ungrateful people. But no. The promise, the hope, the expectation that he will come again is what sustains us. In fact, it is his constant coming to us that enables us to live on here with faith and with hope.

It is good that Jesus ascended. His mission was completed. He gave his all. He deserves to sit at the right hand of the Father in glory. And the reality of his ascension gives us the courage to transcend ourselves and open ourselves to divine contemplation. In Christ's going ahead we are assured that there is a heaven for all of us humans; there is intimacy and at-homeness with the divine. "I go to prepare a place for you." The squalid emptiness of this shrine tells us poignantly that we do not have here what we want, what we are made for, what we long for. We do well to leave it all behind, at least in the desires of our heart, and seek the things that are above. When the light of the ascension illumines our lives, everything is given ultimate meaning. This poor, sun-drenched little space has great meaning because he ascended. And everything else that is human or is made for us humans has meaning because he ascended. The incompleteness of everything is made complete in his ascension as it presages our own ascension. There will be a new heaven and a new earth, because he ascended from earth to heaven and invites each one of us, draws us by his grace, into his ascension. As we pray, we can leave behind the things of earth in his good care and rest in the realities that are above, where we are already one with Christ in his glory. Better yet, we can bring these things along with us into the deifying light, where they can be transformed and renewed and find peace—the peace that the world cannot give, the peace of the risen and ascended Christ.

Our Father . . .

The Descent of the Holy Spirit on the Apostles
Jerusalem: The Upper Room

Once a church, later a mosque with its niche toward Mecca, now just an empty upper room. Emptiness again. Emptiness, crying for fullness. This space has been transformed many times, but perhaps these are the very walls that trembled under the onslaught of a mighty wind as the Holy Spirit transformed her trembling little Church into the powerful missionary force that could obey the departing command of its Founder: go forth and teach all nations. The command has not yet been completely fulfilled. The same Holy Spirit comes upon each of us—at baptism, at confirmation, and each day that we welcome her—and empowers us to live the Christ we are. She empowers us, as she did him who went forth from the Father, to go forth and proclaim, by the way we live as well as in our words, the good news that Jesus is Lord, risen from the dead.

Emptiness. If our lives are too full of care and fear, there is no room for the Spirit, no ear to hear her guiding word. "Cast your care upon the Lord, for he has care of you." If fear still lurks in our hearts at the thought of really being a Christ-person in a world that daily crucifies him in the least of his brethren, we can turn to Mary. She is still in our midst, praying with us, for us.

The question is, Do we really want to be filled with the Holy Spirit, Christ's Spirit, and live a Christ-life? I experience resistance within me. I know that if I do try to live such a life, some will mock me. They will say worse things than that I am drunk at nine in the morning. They will say that I am emotional, naive, fanatical, foolish, misled. This list goes on.

Turn the other cheek. Love enemies. Revere Jews and Palestinians alike. Choose not to stand up for my rights. They will say that I am a weakling and a coward. Yet turning the other cheek takes a lot more courage than fighting back and aggressively getting ahead. Certainly more courage than *I* have. So I need the Holy Spirit. I need her. But I can have her, fully welcome her into my life, only if I am willing to let go of all my own stuff—even my religious and pious stuff. Only when I have gone apart to a higher place, an upper room reached by faith and love, when I have left behind the daily cares and ambitions and even barred the doors, when I have given myself to some fearful prayer, knowing full well my very real weakness and need—only then will the Holy Spirit come in power. And then I can and will go forth with courage and true humanity as well as divinity and bring to others a witness and word of hope.

I sit in the cenacle and know my need. And I know that Mary is here. I can count on her: she will pray with me and for me. We pray as the Church, the whole Church with Mary in our midst. We pray for an ever renewed inpouring of the Spirit upon us all—and, through us, upon a world so in need of the Spirit of peace and love.

Our Father . . .

The Assumption of the Blessed Virgin Mary
Jerusalem: Abbey Church of the Dormition, Mount Zion

This is one of the most peaceful and quiet places in the Holy City—actually, it is just outside the Zion Gate of the Old City—the crypt of the great abbatial church of Dormition Abbey, which crowns the summit of Mount Zion. Here, according to tradition, was the house where Mary dwelt after Jesus' ascension until her own blessed death. It is just around the corner from the cenacle and a short walk from Calvary and other places now filled with sacred memories for the Holy Virgin.

There is a peacefulness in this deep crypt that is most appropriate. The exquisitely serene figure of Mary that lies in repose at the center of the crypt invites us to deeper peace.

On Calvary Mary was given a weighty responsibility: to mother John and all of us—to mother the whole Church. She was with the infant Church in the fear-filled days after the ascension, leading the small but growing community in prayer. After the fearful ones were empowered by the Holy Spirit, Mary's task was easier. But until the end she was the mother-presence within the Church at Jerusalem.

Sometime before the cruel and bitter days of the sixties, Mary completed her earthly ministry and went to sleep in the Lord—only, like her Son, to be quickly awakened. No eyewitness saw his rising, though he appeared to many later. And no eyewitness beheld his mother's resurrection, though she has frequently appeared through the centuries.

Mary was raised up and carried on high by the love of the One who rose and ascended on high. Like Son, like mother. All of us who have been baptized have been baptized into the death and resurrection and ascension of Christ. He is the Firstborn from the dead. We follow, by his powerful love. And first among us followers was Mary.

If Christ has not been raised, our faith is in vain. But Christ *has* been raised. Our faith is *not* in vain. And the Most Faithful One first experienced the fulfillment of her faith and love. We all shall follow.

She is most special. The One who commands us to honor our mothers honors his. He has made her the greatest. And we are privileged, like him and because of him, to have her as our mother.

Mary, it is good to know that your maternal breast is ever here for us to rest upon. How each one of us would have liked to be able to do for our own mothers what Jesus did for you! We can at least rejoice that he did do it for you, our mother in him. You are gone from this earth, most sacred of mothers. And yet you are everywhere present. As we rejoice in the consummation of your wholly human life, we have renewed faith in the consummation of our own lives in and through your Son, our Lord, Jesus.

Mother, heaven does not separate you from us. It only makes you always and everywhere closer. I now rest my head upon your maternal bosom and let your caring love soothe me as I pray. Again, I give myself completely to you. All I want is that all that remains of my life be used exactly as your Son wants.

Our Father . . .

The Coronation of the Blessed Virgin Mary
In the Skies over Israel

We are heading toward 40,000 feet in a clear, very blue sky high above the Mediterranean. This is probably the closest I will get—for a while—to the site of the coronation of Mary as Queen of Heaven and Earth.

As Israel recedes, I wonder what thoughts Mary might have had as the angels bore her aloft for her coronation. Was it so swiftly done that there was little time for thought? Was Mary so lifted up in expectation that she had little thought for what was below? "Forgetting what is behind, press forward toward the mark."

Hardly like a mother. Yes, she was eager to lay eyes again on her Firstborn. But he is the Firstborn of many brothers and sisters. Mary loved the Body of her Son, the little Church, rapidly expanding, seeking to fulfill his final words: "Go forth and teach all nations."

In one sense Mary had fulfilled her most special vocation. It had cost her far more than any poor human heart can comprehend. She had willingly paid the price in full, given all that God asked of her, suffered as only a mother can suffer for her child. Mary certainly earned the merited crown that now awaited her in the heavens. The entire choir of the Kingdom was there to joyfully welcome her. Her ancestors, so proud, were there. Her own mother rejoiced in acknowledgment of a motherhood that made her the grandmother of God and made her daughter God's dearest.

Yet it was in the ecstatic love that impelled Mary into the very heart of the Trinity that she held in deepest maternal care each and every member of her Son—a care that is as real and effective today as it was on that day of assumption and coronation 1,900 years ago. In the very "now" of God it is all one.

It is good—it is awesome—that the most exalted of all women, the gloriously crowned Queen of Heaven and Earth, right this moment and always holds me in her maternal love. With such care, how well I fare. I certainly need never despair. It is a mother's love and care that help hold my childish pettiness and stupid narcissism within limits. A mother's care from a mother who has given us proof of limitless love and care.

I lift my eyes from my own needs. I can leave them in her care. I scan the blue vault that domes the endless fields of clouds. It seems to open to me; I can in some way enter into the joy and exaltation of the heavenly court that celebrates the holy mother of God. It is time to join the unending chorus of the ages: *Ave, Maria, gratia plena. Dominus tecum. Benedicta tu in mulieribus.* Hail, Mary, full of grace. The Lord is with you. Blessed are you among women. Blessed above all creation. You yourself are the crown of all creation, our soiled nature's solitary boast. Our queen, our mother, the glory of Jerusalem—the heavenly Jerusalem as well as that of earth.

Mary, may your sovereignty bring peace to our world. May our hearts find peace in you.

Our Father . . .

7

And There Are Others

Renewal. *Re*-newal: making new again something that already has its place in our rich and precious heritage.

We are living in a time of renewal. The Holy Spirit, through the Second Vatican Council, has called us to renewal. The documents of the council, which were elaborated with much care and prayer, touch on many of the more important facets of our Christian life, exploring them deeply and giving guidance for renewal. But the call to renewal is universal, extending to every aspect of our lives in Christ.

After the council Pope Paul VI, the architect of the renewal, addressed himself particularly to the renewal of our devotion to the Blessed Virgin Mary. His apostolic exhortation *Marialis Cultus* first looked at the relationship between the sacred liturgy and devotion to Mary. Then it set forth some ideas and directives to foster this devotion. The third and final part of the apostolic exhortation was dedicated to the renewal of the rosary. The pope's teaching is simple and clear, noteworthy for its depth and balance. He concludes with this statement: "The rosary is an excellent prayer, but the faithful should feel serenely free in its regard. They should be drawn to its calm recitation by its intrinsic appeal."

The American bishops, undoubtedly inspired by the pope, wrote their own pastoral on the subject. It is called *Behold Your Mother*. In it they, too, show great concern for the renewal of the rosary. In the course of their teaching they offer us this interesting challenge:

> Besides the precise rosary pattern well-known to catholics, we can freely experiment. . . . New sets of mysteries are possible. We have customarily gone from the childhood of Jesus to his passion, bypassing the whole public life. There is rich material here for rosary meditation.

Earlier in this book I suggested some experimental ways in which we might pray the rosary, both as individuals and in groups. Here I would like to respond to the bishops' challenge to consider other sets of mysteries. As I noted in Chapter 2, the fifteen mysteries considered in Chapter 6 were canonized or otherwise authoritatively established only in the fifteenth century, after a long and varied development. In the course of the previous centuries, many other mysteries were considered. I also noted that other forms of the rosary have been formally approved by the Church and are in current use: the rosary of the seven sorrows, the Franciscan Crown, which reflects on Mary's joys, the Bridgettine rosary, and others.

Following the lead of our bishops, and in the spirit of the earlier and richer traditions of our Church, I would like to suggest here some possible sets of mysteries that we might employ. For those who do pray five or fifteen decades of the rosary each day, a broader range of considerations could perhaps enrich their prayer life, bringing them more fully into the mystery of

Christ and bringing him more fully into their daily life. But if you are more comfortable staying with the usual fifteen mysteries, please do so. Remember the words of Pope Paul VI: the faithful should feel serenely free in the way they pray the rosary.

The Mysteries of Christ

As our bishops pointed out, in our usual fifteen mysteries we take a giant leap from Jesus at twelve to Jesus at thirty-six or thirty-seven—twenty-five years that span both his "hidden" life and his active life. There is obviously much food for meditation in these years of our Lord's salvific mission. Listed below are a few sets of mysteries. Although I do not develop my consideration of them at length here, each is pregnant with divine mystery and has much practical teaching for us.

The Hidden Life

1. *Jesus' Submission to Mary and Joseph* (Luke 2:51–52). The wonder of God-become-human humbly obeying two of the fallible creatures that he himself has made.

2. *Jesus Working with Joseph as a Carpenter* (Mark 6:1–6). The humble, helpful apprentice—divine wisdom learning from a man. God working with his hands, knowing blisters and splinters, an aching back and a sweaty brow.

3. *Jesus Within the Extended Family* (Matt. 13:53–58). God living such an ordinary life in the village that no one noticed him—he seemed like just one more villager.

4. *The Death of Joseph.* Scripture only implicitly tells us of this. Jesus knew what it was to be the only son of a widow.

5. *Jesus' Parting from Mary* (Matt. 12:46–50). A painful but challenging and loving separation—for our sake.

Jesus' Encounters with Mary

1. *Cana* (John 2:1–12). He cannot say no, nor can he say the child's yes. No codependency here.

2. *Jesus' Visit to Nazareth* (Luke 4:16–30). Moments of maternal pride and moments of maternal terror and heartbreak for a loving Relative and Friend.

3. *"Here are my mother and my brothers".* (Matt. 12:46–50). Perhaps only Mary understood that it was not a rejection.

4. *"Blessed the womb that bore you"* (Luke 11:27–28). Again, the Most Faithful One understood.

5. *At the Cross.* (John 19:25–27). We all have a mother in Mary, who gave birth to us in agony.

Jesus' Ministry to Other Women

1. *The Woman Who Touched His Garment* (Matt. 9:20–22). A cruelly induced shame made her hide, but she could not hide from Love. Her faith made her shine.

2. *Jairus' Daughter* (Mark 5:21–43). Such power, such dignity, such humanity in this Healer.

3. *The Widow of Nain* (Luke 7:11–17). Some needs speak for themselves. A mother needs her only son; yet for love of us, he deprived his own mother.

4. *The Adulterous Woman* (John 8:3–11). Where was the man? Jesus would not stand for such injustice.

5. *"She has shown such great love"* (Luke 7:36–50). Love is what matters, and Jesus let women show their love in a woman's way.

Table Talk

1. *At Levi's* (Matt. 9:9–13). He came for us sinners.

2. *At Simon's* (Luke 7:36–50). Love is what matters.

3. *At Bethany* (Luke 10:38–42). There are different vocations.

4. *Again at Bethany* (John 12:1–8). Jesus wants us to wait on him.

5. *At the Cenacle* (John 13–17). Jesus pours out his heart and gives us the gift of himself in the Eucharist.

The Healing Mysteries

1. *At Peter's* (Matt. 8:14–17). Jesus has complete command over sickness.

2. *The Man Lowered Through the Roof by His Friends* (Mark 2:1–12). Jesus listens to the prayers of friends.

3. *The Man with the Withered Hand* (Mark 3:1–6). Jesus is angry when we play games and use others.

4. *The Ten Lepers* (Luke 17:11–19). Jesus is sensitive to gratitude.

5. *The Blind Man at Jericho* (Mark 10:46–52). Jesus is not put off by our importunate cries.

"I Am": Jesus' Self-Identity

1. *"I am the Bread of Life"* (John 6:35).

2. *"I am the Gate"* (John 10:9).

3. *"I am the Good Shepherd"* (John 10:14).

4. *"I am the Way: I am Truth and Life"* (John 14:6).

5. *"I am the True Vine"* (John 15:1).

The Resurrection Mysteries

Every Sunday we celebrate the resurrection of our Lord — the central mystery of our faith. On Sundays, especially during the paschal time, we might like to dwell more fully on the resurrection, either in its foretypes or in itself.

The Foretypes of the Resurrection

1. *Elijah Raises the Widow's Only Son* (1 Kings 17:17–24).

2. *Elisha Raises the Son of the Shunamite* (2 Kings 4:8–37).

3. *Jonah Comes Forth from the Whale After Three Days and Nights* (Jon. 2:1–11).

4. *Jesus Raises the Son of the Widow of Nain* (Luke 7:11–17). Jesus himself is the only son of a widow.

5. *Jesus Raises Lazarus* (John 11:1–44).

Jesus' Resurrection

1. *On the Road to Emmaus* (Luke 24:13–35). "We had hoped . . ." — the Scriptures as a source of hope.

2. *Easter Night* (Luke 24:36–43). "Have you anything here to eat?" — the humanity of Jesus.

3. *A Week Later* (John 20:24–29). "Blessed are those who have not seen and yet believe."

4. *By the Sea* (John 21:1–23). Peter is humbled that he might be exalted.

5. *On Olivet* (Luke 24:50–53). Go tell all that he will return.

Our Sacramental Life

Praying the rosary meditating on the sacraments may help us to enter more and more fully into the sacramental life of the Church. The rosary might in this way be used as part of our immediate preparation to receive a particular sacrament.

The Sacraments

1. *Baptism* (Mark 1:9–11). Baptism makes us, too, the beloved children of God as the Holy Spirit comes upon us.

2. *Confirmation* (Acts 2:1–4). A new power is given us to live the Christ-life fearlessly and to bring the good news powerfully to others.

3. *Eucharist* (Luke 22:19–20). A *memoria*—a memory that is a reality; here we offer perfect worship to the Father.

4. *Reconciliation* (John 20:19–23). The first gift of our risen Lord, a sacrament of peace.

5. *Anointing* (James 5:13–18). We the Church continue the healing ministry of Christ.

The Eucharist

1. *The Manna in the Wilderness* (Exod. 16:4–36). Sweetness on a hard journey—but just enough for each day.

2. *Cana* (John 2:1–12). Water becomes wine as wine will become blood to celebrate our divine nuptials.

3. *The Multiplication of the Loaves* (John 6:1–15). In the hands of the apostles and their successors, there is food for all.

4. *The Last Supper* (Mark 14:22–25). This is my body. This is my blood.

5. *The Meal at Emmaus* (Luke 24:28–32). They recognized him in the breaking of the bread.

Reconciliation

1. *"Though your sins are like scarlet, they shall be white as snow"* (Isa. 1:18).

2. *"A broken, contrite heart you never scorn"* (Ps. 51:19).

3. *"Her sins, many as they are, have been forgiven her, because she has shown such great love"* (Luke 7:47).

4. *"Neither do I condemn you"* (John 8:11).

5. *"Father, forgive them; they do not know what they are doing"* (Luke 23:34).

Anointing of the Sick

1. *Peter's Mother-in-Law* (Matt. 8:14–15). Jesus came into the house, and the fever left her.

2. *The Centurion's Servant* (Matt. 8:5–13). "Sir, I am not worthy to have you under my roof."

3. *The Leper* (Mark 1:40–45). "Jesus stretched out his hand and touched him."

4. *The Official from Capernaum* (John 4:46–54). "Unless you see signs and portents you will not believe."

5. *The Commission* (Mark 6:7–13). The Twelve were sent to anoint those who are sick.

On the Journey

As we continue on the journey of life toward the Kingdom, we are at different times deeply immersed in particular experiences or concerns. At such times it can be very helpful during our rosary to meditate on mysteries that are relevant to where we are. Here are just a few examples.

Vocation

In our teenage years and at other transition periods in our lives, the question of vocation—what we want to do with our lives with the Lord—looms very large. But even at other times, clarity and fidelity are challenging and important.

1. *The Search* (John 1:35–39). "Come and see."

2. *The Call* (Mark 1:17–20). "Come after me."

3. *Fidelity* (Luke 9:57–62). Those who look back are not worthy.

4. *Betrayal* (Matt. 26:47–50). Betraying the Son of man with a kiss.

5. *Fidelity to the End* (John 21:18–22). "You are to follow me."

Contemplative Mysteries

Sometimes we are drawn more deeply into the awesome presence of God and sense that thoughts and images will only get in the way. At such times we might simply abide with those mysterious manifestations of the Lord that we find in the book of Revelation.

1. *The Alpha and the Omega* (Rev. 1:8).

2. *The Lion of Judah* (Rev. 5:5).

3. *The Son of Man* (Rev. 14:14).

4. *The King of Kings* (Rev. 17:14).

5. *The Morning Star* (Rev. 22:16).

Pregnancy

One of the most special times in the life of a couple is when they are pregnant with new life. To live this time in close union with the God who hid himself within a womb, as well as with Mary and Joseph, can greatly enrich the experience and bring comfort and support during hours of fear and concern.

1. *Mary's Conception* (Luke 1:26–38). Mary knows all the mixed emotions that arise with the announcement, "You are going to have a baby."

2. *Mary Visits Elizabeth and John* (Luke 1:38–56). Mary and Jesus are eager to come to mother and child to bring joy and help.

3. *Mary Gives Birth to Her Son* (Luke 2:1–20). The time, the place, and the manner are in God's providence; the caring angels will be there.

4. *Giving Birth* (John 16:21). There will be pain—Jesus knows—and then there will be great joy.

5. *Mary Presents Her Son to the Father* (Luke 2:22–38). Every child belongs to God; the child's and the parents' future is in his all-powerful hands.

When We Are in Mourning

At a time of mourning, whatever be the cause of our loss, we do well to turn to the God of all consolation. His compassion for us in our needs is touchingly manifested in his deeds.

1. *The Widow of Nain* (Luke 7:11–17). No one had to ask on behalf of this widow, yet she received one of Jesus' greatest miracles.

2. *At the Tomb of Lazarus* (John 11:1–44). "See how he loved him." This Strong Man was not afraid to shed tears.

3. *The Death of His Cousin John* (Matt. 14:1–13). At times we need to go apart and be with our grief.

4. *The Weeping Women* (Luke 23:27–31). He leads us to a deeper understanding of our human misery, and he is with us in it.

5. *Mary and John on Calvary* (John 19:25–27). Not even the depths of his own suffering can hold back his compassion for us in our need.

These are but a few of the many possible sets of mysteries that we can bring together to make the rosary a more integral part of our daily life. You undoubtedly have passages of the Scriptures—perhaps particular gospel stories—that have touched you deeply at one time or another. Do not hesitate to meditate upon these as you pray the decades. Your continued daily reading of, or rather, listening to the Gospels and other parts of the sacred Scriptures will add to your personal hoard of spiritual food. Again and again you can savor that which is most sweet or most nourishing for you as you finger the beads. Let your daily rosary be a place of deeply personal encounter with Christ in his mysteries.

8

Mary's Beads

The rosary is constantly hailed as a great Marian devotion, yet it is quite Christocentric and also has a trinitarian aspect. We begin "in the name of the Father and of the Son and of the Holy Spirit." We then profess our faith: "I believe in God, the Father almighty . . . and in Jesus Christ, his only Son. . . . I believe in the Holy Spirit. . . ." And we end each decade with the Doxology: "Glory be to the Father and to the Son and to the Holy Spirit. . . ." Each decade begins with the prayer that Jesus taught us, again addressed to the Father.

When we do hail Mary, it is because she is full of grace, the grace of Christ her Son. She is worthy to be hailed because she has found favor with God; she is God's favored one. She is blessed because of the fruit of her womb, Jesus.

As we pray these prayers, we ponder on the mysteries of Christ. It is *his* annunciation, birth, and presentation that we contemplate. It is finding *him* that gives us joy. It is *his* passion that we ponder from the garden to Calvary. It is *his* resurrection and ascension that give us the hope of glory. Mary's glory is wholly consequent on his.

If we do ask Mary to pray for us—and we certainly do—while we ponder on these mysteries, it is first of all that she might help us to enter into them and understand them more fully. She actually participated in each one of them in a most unique and special way.

The annunciation of the coming of Christ the Savior was made to Mary, and—great mystery—its actualization was made dependent on her consent. She was the one who carried Jesus to Elizabeth and John. She was the one who gave birth, from whom Jesus was born. She was the one purified at his presentation, even as she presented him; the one who received the prophecies. She was the one who searched for him and found him. She saw the effects of the agony, scourging, and crowning as only a mother could. She walked with him to Calvary and stood by him there—by him not only physically but in a total communion of spirit: it was her Son whom he offered. We do not know what was this woman of faith's experience of the risen Lord, but we do know that she was the strong support in the midst of a fearful group of the faithful awaiting the grace and courage of Pentecost. And so she received her due reward.

Mary lived these mysteries—in herself and in her Son. She knew the inner responses, feelings, and attitudes of her Son as no one else could. She watched him closely through many years and understood him with the intuition of a mother. She spent many, many hours in conversation with him. Together they shared prayer and the Scriptures. Yes, there were things she did not understand, but she pondered all these things in her heart. This woman, who had been overshadowed and made fruitful by the Spirit, listened deeply to that Spirit as she pondered. Her insights and intuitions were deep, and we ask her to share them with us as we pray.

We are poor sinners: "Pray for us sinners." We have a compassionate and loving Savior. But he is a man. He is God. Isn't there something about a mother—an understanding that naturally reassures us? A mother forgives. A mother kisses and makes whole. A mother does not miss the little things. Mother is our natural intercessor with Father. And this mother cannot be denied. Remember Cana: Jesus cannot say no to her even when he seems to want to. A watchful mother, she sees needs even before we do—again, Cana—and takes care of them effectively. No wonder we ask her to do the asking for us now—each and every *now* and that most important *now*, the ultimate *now* for us: the hour of our death.

What we ask of Mary is that in her being to her Son and with him to his Father, she bring us with her—ourselves and all our needs. She is wholly centered on her Son, and she wants us likewise to be so. We certainly do not want her to turn from her Son to us. She knows far better than we that we are one with her Son, because we have been baptized into Christ. When she attends now to us she attends to him, in his needs. He no longer has needs that demand her maternal care, except in us. In us, she cares for him.

It is hard to see how anyone could think that in turning to Mary, in praying to Mary, we in some way turn from her Son, detract from the honor due to him. How can prayer to Mary ever compete with prayer to her Son? If we poor sinners have become one with Christ, how much more so she. When we turn to Mary, we always see Christ—her God and her Son.

Jesus tells us that he always did the things that pleased the Father, and it was his Father who laid down the command: Honor your mother. With all his heart, and one with his Father, he fulfilled this command. He preserved her from all sin; he endowed her with a fullness of grace, with a faith that called forth prophetic praise: blessed is she who believed. He allowed her, from the presentation up to Calvary, to share most deeply in his salvific sufferings. In the end he made her partaker in his resurrection and ascension and, as he promised in the book of Revelation (3:21), he invited her to share his throne even as he shares his Father's throne in the Kingdom. Jesus has done all that he can to honor his mother. And he takes delight when anyone honors her, just as we take delight when our own mothers are honored. Indeed, if our call is to be one with Christ and to think as he does, to see things as he does, to value things as he does, to act as he does, then we are called to honor Mary, and honor her as much as we can. This is the Christ thing, the Christian thing.

The practice of the rosary invites us to spend time each day with Mary, to allow her to teach us more about her Son. It reminds us that we can count on her as a mother—a mother given to us on Calvary. We are her children in virtue of the bitterest of birth pangs. And it gives us an opportunity to honor her with Christ, to salute her as his chosen queen. Fittingly, then, do we end our rosary "Hail, holy Queen."

9

A Closing Word:
Into the Next Century

As day by day the news came to us, it was hard to believe that it was not a television series: The Berlin Wall was breached and quickly fell. Nations, one after the other, threw off the communist dictatorships that had shackled them for decades and chose new leaders and a new approach to life. An age-old religious faith refound its freedom — even in Russia. A new day was dawning for millions. It will be a day filled with economic struggle and lots of work for all, but the essential turn has taken place. There has been a conversion from an avowed atheism to a recognition that, as Gorbachev declared, religious faith and the religious institution have roles to play in creating a healthy society.

We were astonished at this sudden turnabout. But should we have been? We have been praying for it for a long time. Do we really believe in the power of our prayer? At Fatima Mary promised that if we prayed the rosary and gave Russia into her care, the change would come. We prayed the rosary. The popes and the bishops consecrated Russia and the world to Mary. And the change has come.

As the struggle between atheistic communism and the Christian West (which, unfortunately, in many ways is far from the mind and heart of Christ in its values) drew to a close, there seemed to emerge for us a new hope for peace. But then we were abruptly brought to the realization that the confrontation that has absorbed so much of our attention in recent decades was but a parenthesis within a centuries-old struggle between Islam and the Judeo-Christian world. This struggle, which continued offstage while we were absorbed in the conflict with the forces of atheistic communism, has once more come to the fore, threatening devastation.

In light of this ongoing struggle, we are coming to realize that the new visits of Mary, Our Lady of Peace, at Medugorje address themselves to this ancient and massive threat. As Mary urges a true conversion of heart, along with prayer and fasting, the villages of Medugorje—in company with thousands of pilgrims—nightly pray the fifteen decades. It is while the community is praying the rosary that Mary comes and speaks to her chosen ones. In 1571, as mighty forces of Islam prepared to invade Christian Europe, the saintly pontiff Pius V called upon all the people to take up the rosary. Two years later the pope established the Feast of the Holy Rosary to commemorate gratefully the day, October 7, 1571, when the Muslim armada was devastated at Lepanto. It was a victory for the rosary: the rosary had saved Europe.

We have come to a point in the development of armaments that war has to become unthinkable: armaments have to become something obsolete, belonging to a benighted past. The inconceivable destruction and loss of life that today's chemical, biological, and nuclear weapons can bring about in a matter of minutes makes the use of them—and even the threat or plan to use them—a crime against humanity. No one knows what kind of fallout such use would entail. Indeed, any country that uses them might, in the end, be the one that suffers most from them as their residue seeps back slowly to poison the atmosphere and infect the population with a living death. Apart from these effects, which are almost too horrible to think about, is the fact that the continued production of weaponry, and its maintenance and disposal, is destroying the economy of the entire world. So much of human genius and our God-given resources cannot be dedicated to what any sane person hopes and prays will end up in a trash heap—a very expensive trash heap—without severely impoverishing us all. We cannot continue to live with a wartime economy, but we do not seem to know how to change to a peacetime economy. Yet the needs of the homeless, the hungry, and the uneducated of our own nation and of the world cry out to us for creative and life-giving use of our potential.

Mary places in our hands a weapon for peace: the rosary. It is a weapon that every man, woman, and child can take up. It is a weapon that we, like the Israelites of old, can hold in one hand while we are busy reconstructing a safe world with the other. When there is so much hopelessness abroad, the rosary is a source of hope. It takes us through the apparently devastating defeat of All Goodness to the triumph of resurrection and ascension and ultimate glorification. It tells us that we have a Lord in heaven who loves us and has given us the greatest sign of love: "No one can have greater love than to lay down his life for his friends." It tells us, too, that there is at his side a woman, a mother, who gets what she wants.

Mary told us at Fatima how to bring down the walls of an atheistic empire that threatened the peace of all. And when we responded, the wall of Berlin came down faster than the walls of Jericho before the trumpets of Joshua. When prayer, the rosary, brings down walls, it furthers peace and unity. In less time than anyone ever conceived possible, the German people were reunited. And even more wondrous: the man who had been the leader of the threatening forces of atheistic communism was given the West's highest recognition of an agent of peace, the Nobel Peace Prize—the same prize that was given only a few years earlier to Mother Teresa of Calcutta, who brings peace through prayer and care.

Mary has promised us peace as the fruit of prayer and conversion. Praying the rosary, we enter, with her help, ever more deeply into the mysteries of Christ, her Son. This can only lead us to a true inner conversion. Our hearts are turned to him who so loves us and who loves each one of our sisters and brothers in this world. He loves each of them enough to have died for them. Must we not also love them and strive with all our being for their peace and ours, for their prosperity and well-being? The rosary is a prayer of conversion, a prayer that converts.

Peace is our great concern, for it is a question of survival—the survival of the human race. But there will never be peace without social justice. As long as a parent sees his or her children suffering, homeless, or hungry while others are wasting the fat of the land, the bounty that the Lord meant for all, there cannot be peace in his heart and there will not be peace on earth.

We need to meditate on the mysteries of social justice:

1. *Jesus Feeds the Hungry* (John 6:1–15). God has never failed to feed the hungry. It is the politics of food that causes starvation. We need the political will to share our God-given bounty.

2. *Jesus Heals the Sick* (Mark 1:32–34). Not in hospitals but in the streets where the homeless are, the tormented ones who suffer in mind as well as in body, Jesus offers healing.

3. *Jesus Respects Women* (John 8:3–11). He accepts not just those whom others find "respectable."

4. *Jesus Reaches Out and Touches Outcasts* (Mark 1:40–45). PWAs (People with AIDs) are among the lepers of our day. AIDS is depriving much of Africa of a whole generation of creative leadership.

5. *Jesus Honors the Despised* (Luke 10:29–37). The Palestinians are today's Samaritans, despised most by those who have themselves long been the victims. And let us not forget the blacks, the gays, the hispanics, and the many immigrant groups.

There are many other mysteries that we could meditate upon under the guidance of the woman who belonged to an oppressed and subjugated people, who was displaced and fled into exile, who as a teenager dared to sing in the presence of the priestly rulers:

> The Almighty has used the power of his arm,
>   he has routed the arrogant of heart.
> He has pulled down princes from their thrones
>   and raised high the lowly.
> He has filled the starving with good things,
>   sent the rich away empty.
>   *—Luke 1:51–53*

We still need to meditate on Mary's own experiences: on unwed motherhood, on a perilous errand of care, on a displaced and exiled family, on prophecies of doom, on a "runaway" lost in the big city.

We still need the strength and consolation of a crucified love, of an empty tomb, of ultimate victory. We need the Holy Spirit, with her empowering gifts of wisdom, understanding, knowledge, counsel, fortitude, piety, and reverence. We need her fruits of love, joy, peace, patience, kindness, benignity, long-suffering, and the reverence of chaste love. We need the pledge enfleshed in the victory over death and glorification of one of us. Not only God ascends as the one who descended. He ascends as the first of many. Already Mary and the others who rose with him have followed. We, too, shall follow.

And so we go on into the possibilities of the twenty-first century with a hope that can overcome even death, a hope that we daily renew by praying the rosary.

A Select Bibliography

Burnside, Eleanor T. *Bible Rosary: The Life of Jesus—Thirty-Five Mysteries*. Birmingham, MI: Rosary Thirty-Five, 1981.

De Montfort, St. Louis. *The Secret of the Rosary*. Translated by Mary Baerbour. Bay Shore, NY: Montfort Father, 1954.

Haffert, John M. *Sex and the Mysteries*. Washington, NJ: Ave Maria Institute, 1970.

London, Larry. *The Seven-Day Scriptural Rosary*. Huntington, IN: Our Sunday Visitor, 1988.

Marcucci, Domenico *Through the Rosary with Fra Angelico*. New York: Alba House, 1987.

Paul VI. *Devotion to the Blessed Virgin Mary: Marialis Cultus*. Washington, D.C.: United States Catholic Conference, 1974.

Ward, J. Neville. *Five for Sorrow, Ten for Joy: A Consideration of the Rosary*. New York: Doubleday, 1973.

White, Bob. *The Prayer of the Heart: An Introduction to the Rosary* (unpublished manuscript).

Wilkins, Eithne. *The Rose-Garden Game: A Tradition of Beads and Flowers*. New York: Herder & Herder, 1969.

William, Franz Michael. *The Rosary: Its History and Meaning*. Translated by Edwin Kaiser. New York: Benziger, 1953.